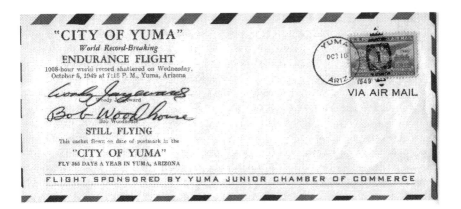

Commemorative airmail envelope celebrating the breaking of the world endurance record.

THE LONGEST FLIGHT

Yuma's Quest for the Future: Sixty Years Later

SHIRLEY WOODHOUSE MURDOCK
AND
JAMES A. GILLASPIE

iUniverse, Inc.
NEW YORK   BLOOMINGTON

The Longest Flight
Yuma's Quest for the Future: Sixty Years Later

iUniverse books may be ordered through booksellers or by contacting:

iUniverse
1663 Liberty Drive
Bloomington, IN 47403
www.iuniverse.com
1-800-Authors (1-800-288-4677)

Because of the dynamic nature of the Internet, any Web addresses or links contained in this book
may have changed since publication and may no longer be valid.

ISBN: 978-1-4401-7358-5 (sc)
ISBN: 978-1-4401-7360-8 (dj)
ISBN: 978-1-4401-7359-2 (ebk)

Library of Congress Control Number: 2009936412

Printed in the United States of America

iUniverse rev. date: 9/29/2009

Also by Shirley Woodhouse Murdock and James A. Gillaspie:

The Longest Flight: Yuma's Quest for the Future

Also by Shirley Woodhouse Murdock:

The Mules Go in Front: A Story of Hardship & Triumph Along Arizona's Lower Gila

In memory of

Paul Burch.

He was many things to many people,

husband, father, friend, mentor, teacher, gentleman,

and one darn good airplane mechanic, who knew no
bounds.

The success of the endurance flight was his like no other.

CONTENTS

PREFACE

The story of the Yuma endurance flight of 1949 has remained an important memory to me. It was exciting having my brother, Bob, involved in a flight that received worldwide attention.

In the mid-1980s, I began writing a book of regional history (*Roll, Arizona and the Mohawk Valley*) and stories about our parents' pioneering days and their flying experiences, which included a chapter about the endurance flight, because it was a Woodhouse family flying story.

Then, about 1997, as the fiftieth anniversary of the flight approached and the *City of Yuma* airplane was found, purchased by the Yuma Jaycees, and brought back "home" for restoration, I began to gather stories of that enterprise. It soon became obvious to me that I should expand that original chapter and write about the people who were spending hundreds of hours and, in a few cases, thousands of hours restoring the airplane and showing it around town at major events to raise funds for the restoration. Jim Gillaspie, who was the kingpin ("technical advisor") in the restoration of the airplane, was able to educate me regarding that major work. He is a historian and enjoys researching and writing, particularly about aviation history. Eventually, I asked him to be a co-author with me. Only after a repeat of that offer did he accept that role.

It has been a pleasure to talk with a number of old-timers or their sons and daughters. I've had to ask some of them to relive the pain of losing their fathers, but they've all come back with amusing, poignant stories. There is still a great deal of appreciation for what those pilots, refueling crew members, and hundreds of other supporters did for the city of Yuma sixty years ago. It is hoped that, through this book and the activities of the present-day workers, that appreciation will enfold many more Yumans.

Shirley Woodhouse Murdock

PREFACE

This edition of *The Longest Flight* is the third printing. The first printing of one thousand copies was in 1999 and the second in 2001. The books, which covered events from 1949 through the first half of 1999, sold very well. They soon became collectors' items, selling through dealers on half.com for as much as fifteen times the original retail price.

Based on the success of the earlier books and the need to tell the rest of the story, at least up to the sixtieth anniversary of the event, we decided to publish this new book.

Endurance is defined as "the power of enduring, specifically the ability to last, continue, or remain, and the ability to stand pain, distress, and fatigue." When one looks up the word "endure," one finds that it means "to harden the heart." It is one thing to endure when an unfortunate situation occurs, but it is quite another to volunteer to put oneself in harm's way. Every one of these words directly relates to what Woody and Bob had to do for no greater individual gain than to be able to say, "We hardened the heart; we persevered." This is the stuff of heroes. Although they didn't realize it at the time, the pain, distress, and fatigue that they placed on their bodies would stay with them the rest of their lives. To touch on one area, the act of flying in a light aircraft without proper ear protection is detrimental even for just a few hours, but that was the way it was done in those days. People today think they are abused if they have to stay in a small plane for five hours or a commercial airliner for fifteen hours—but none of this compares to what the *City of Yuma*'s pilots endured.

Woody and Bob, between them, lifted over fifty-two thousand pounds of fuel into that airplane while leaning halfway out of the airplane in the slipstream. They endured the stress of flying at night, ever alert to the sound of the engine and thinking, "What do I do if the engine quits? Where do I try to put it down?" The refueling runs, as beautiful as they were to see, were potential sources of danger. They were not just gently floating with the winds without a care.

We have written this book, not only to honor those of the past, but also for the generations to come so they can have one more reason to be proud of their heritage. The story had to be told.

James A. Gillaspie

CHAPTER ONE

THE ROOTS OF AVIATION IN YUMA, INCLUDING ENDURANCE FLIGHTS

ROBERT G. FOWLER, FIRST MAN TO FLY AN AIRPLANE INTO THE STATE OF ARIZONA

Although not widely known, Yuma has a history of endurance flights dating back to 1911. Yuma was the take-off point for a flight by Robert G. "Bob" Fowler that set the world's record for duration and distance covered in 1911. Bob Fowler had entered the first Transcontinental Air Race, in which William Randolph Hearst's *American* offered fifty thousand dollars to "the first man who could fly across the American continent within thirty consecutive days and complete the journey by October 10, 1911." Fowler's airplane was a Cole Flyer, a Model B pusher-type biplane built at the Wright Brothers plant in Dayton, Ohio, where he went and had some three hours of instruction and ordered the airplane shipped to San Francisco. He had many troubles along the way, including a crash in Colfax, California, and one in the snow at Donner Lake in the Sierra Nevada Mountains. From there, the Flyer was shipped to Los Angeles by freight train. It was repaired, and he started all over again. On that second attempt, he took off from Ascot Park in Los Angeles on October 10, exactly thirty-eight years before the *City of Yuma* landed after its long flight and the very day that he had hoped to reach the east coast. More delays occurred, one caused by Los Angeles fog, which forced him to land at night at Tournament Park in Pasadena. He then had a "blown-up engine" at Banning, California.

Finally, on October 24, he took off from Mecca, near the Salton Sea, and arrived in Yuma on October 25. His arrival was expected. Two thousand breathless spectators had assembled in the Yuma ballpark. They first saw a small speck over Pilot Knob. It grew to the size of a bird and then a full-sized airplane. The crowd watched the wonderful object circle the enclosure and make a graceful landing almost on home plate. Bob was the first birdman to visit Yuma; the Cole Flyer was the first flying machine in the city and the first airplane to enter Arizona under its own power and not riding in a boxcar. "Everyone from all over the valley was there," wrote Madeline Spain, who witnessed the great event. "We had been waiting for days, and the birdman's arrival was real exciting." Fowler then clattered into Maricopa on October 29 and landed alongside the railroad tracks across the street from the main post office. It had been a nonstop flight from Yuma (four hours and twenty-six minutes) and the 165-mile trip won him a world's record for duration and distance covered. Ruth M. Reinhold related this in her book *Sky Pioneering*.

In June of 1929, former residents of Yuma, Martin and Margaret (Peg) Jensen, along with William Ulbrich, attempted to break the world's refueling record of 172 hours, 32 minutes, and 6 seconds. This record attempt, made in a Bellanca aircraft flying over Roosevelt Field, New York, ended after only seventy hours due to a fuel problem. The existing record at that time, established at Ft. Worth, Texas, was held by Reg Robbins and James Kelly.

LEO, THE MGM LION

Martin Jensen and his wife were quite well known in Yuma, having been the subject of various headlines in the local newspaper. They were married in a Jenny while flying above Yuma in 1925. Martin was an aviation barnstormer, having come in second in a race to be the first to fly to Hawaii. In 1927 he was involved in an accident, described by Ruth M. Reinhold in her book *Sky Pioneering* as being the most bizarre incident in Arizona's aeronautical history: a plane crash with Leo, MGM Pictures' African lion mascot. Martin, flying a specially modified Ryan B-1 Brougham with Leo aboard, crashed in Arizona's Mazatzal Mountains, but both survived. The lion was being flown across the country with planned stops along the way as a publicity stunt for MGM.

Father of the late Jackie Griffen of Yuma, Ham Eubank, and another cowboy, Lewis Bowman, were working cattle in a rough canyon in the area when Ham's horse shied and started bucking. Ham got off and looked around to determine what had frightened his horse. He discovered the wrecked airplane with Leo in it. The pilot had walked away, hiking for two and one-half days in the rough country before reaching a ranch. The area in which the crash occurred is known as Hell's Gate, and is some of the most remote and isolated terrain in Arizona. A group of intrepid cowboys improvised a sled from a forked oak and, using frightened mules, eventually rescued Leo from the area. He was transported to Phoenix by truck and to Los Angeles by train. The story is detailed in Frank V. Gillette's book, *Pleasant Valley.*

The *City of Yuma* flying at one thousand feet over the Colorado River, heading north, looking back on the city of Yuma.

In 1949 the Yuma Jaycee-sponsored world-record endurance flight touched the lives of most, if not all, of the nine thousand people in Yuma. For those directly involved, it was the adventure of a lifetime, something to be proud of and not to be forgotten. As the years rolled by, memories faded and the stories took on new meaning. Among the old-timers, Bob Hodge loved to tell amusing stories about the flight to anyone who would take the time to listen. Horace Griffen's main topic of conversation concerns the flight. He has made numerous public appearances in which he describes details of the flight. He has also kept in contact with most of the principal players and was instrumental in putting on a fortieth anniversary celebration of the landing in 1989. He didn't know it, but he was destined to play an important part in the continuing story of Yuma's endurance flight.

FLY FIELD

Yuma International Airport, as we now know it, can trace its roots to 1925. This was the year that key individuals with a keen vision for future air transportation were appointed to the Yuma Chamber of Commerce aviation committee. This committee, which was chaired by Judge Peter T. Robertson and included Everett Johnson and E. C. Briegger, went to work to secure an airport or landing field for Yuma. In approximately two years, these men were able to secure certain appropriated land (forty acres) from the government and have it cleared and leveled. They also gained the aid and influence of the Yuma Valley Country Club; secured the offer of a thirty-two thousand dollar hangar delivered FOB, Yuma; and obtained legislation authorizing the board of supervisors to make expenditures in the establishment and maintenance of public aviation fields. Through their efforts, the forty-acre plot of sand was officially designated as an active airport. This designation was made possible through the efforts of the committee assisted by Col. Ben Franklin Fly. The airport, Fly Field, was subsequently named after Col. Fly to honor him for his efforts to bring about the Yuma Mesa Project. In fact, he was often referred to as "the daddy of the Yuma Mesa Project." In an April 28, 1928, issue of *Politics,* the colonel, who initiated the legislation in Washington and carried it to a triumphant conclusion, was dubbed the "premier of all parliamentary solicitors." His efforts resulted in an unfailing supply of water to irrigate 130,000 acres of land. He also obtained funding of 12.5 million dollars, which represented the initial funding for the construction of Laguna Dam.

Fly Field was a start, but it had many shortcomings including the loose sand and the lack of facilities. In fact, Lt. R. N. Goddard, flyer from Imperial, California, in an address to the American Legion in 1926, declared that most of the flyers from San Diego and other aviation fields passed up Yuma when flying over because of the soft sand, which could cause an airplane to flip upside down. This problem, and the fact that in September 1926 a New York aviation company designated Yuma as one of the line ports for a mail route from New York to San Diego, was not lost on the aviation committee. The committee felt that they needed at least 160 acres, and some of that land would have to be bought. The rest would come from a trade with the government and a second trade with the Yuma Valley Country Club. The government was willing to go into negotiations because of the importance of having a safe and adequate landing field at Yuma. In fact, the Second Division Air Corps at Fort Sam Houston, on behalf of the government, offered to give Fly Field a steel-frame hangar capable of housing twelve airplanes. The Country Club was willing to trade some of its property for adjoining land that had been set aside by the government. The chamber named a special committee to work with the aviation committee to put through to fruition a first-class landing field in Yuma. This special committee consisted of: E. F. Sanguinetti, Norman Adair, Bert Caudry, Dr. H. D. Ketcherside, L. M. White, C. E. Potter, A. N. Kelly, Joseph Corey, William Wisener, F. W. Cresswell, and Frank Elliot.

The committee looked to the Yuma County Board of Supervisors to make appropriations for acquiring the rest of the land. The supervisors were authorized by House Bill No. 51 to make expenditures for establishing public aviation fields. This bill, which was passed and signed during a prior legislature, was introduced by Representative William Wisener of Yuma County in the interest of the development of Fly Field. The board subsequently set aside seven thousand dollars for improvements to the airfield.

Judge Robertson had lobbied for over ten years and carried on correspondence with key government agencies to keep alive the theme that Yuma belonged on the aviation map. The fruits of his labor were starting to pay off. The aviation committee had received official recognition from the War Department. The *Yuma Morning Sun* announced on November 13, 1927, that the government had allocated 640 acres of land to be used for a local flying field to the aviation committee of the Yuma Chamber of Commerce. The article further stated that the new field was about four miles south of the center of the city on the main highway to Phoenix. Fly Field, consisting of forty acres, named for Col. B. F. Fly, was abandoned and the name transferred to the new field. Work started the following day on the clearing of 160 acres. During the last week of December 1927, Lt. Harry Waddington, who for some time worked with the aviation committee, made the first landing on the new field.

On December 15, 1927, Congressman Douglas of Arizona introduced a bill asking for the lease of 640 acres of government land to Yuma County for twenty years at a cost of one dollar per year. Simultaneously, a bill known as the Ashurst bill was working its way through the senate. This bill was drawn up by Judge Robertson. If passed, it would allow all counties in Arizona equal treatment by the government, that is, they would be able to lease government land for airport purposes and at the same rate.

People in Yuma were elated. Aviation officials predicted that, as a result of the passage of this action, it wouldn't be long until a postal route was established between San Diego and Dallas since the southern route offered ideal flying weather with little mountainous terrain.

The next course of action for the committee was to urge early acquisition of two emergency fields in eastern Yuma County, one at Tacna or Wellton, and the other at Aztec. At that time, it was necessary to have an emergency field along every fifty miles of an air route.

President Calvin Coolidge signed the Yuma Aviation Bill on February 27, 1928. Terms of the lease were for twenty years at one dollar per year with the privilege of renewal for another twenty years at the same rate. A special act of Congress was necessary to grant the secretary of the interior authority to lease the land. The act provided that the United States agencies "shall have access to the field and that, in times of emergency, the government shall have the right to assume control."

TRANSCONTINENTAL AIR RACES

Almost immediately, the aviation committee started lining up activities for the airport. Yuma was picked to be a night stop on three men's classes of transcontinental air races from New York to Los Angeles and an international air race from Mexico to Los Angeles. These airplanes were expected to arrive in Yuma starting September 9, 1928. The chamber agreed to give one thousand dollars lap money and provide free gas and oil to the racers, which was estimated to cost two thousand dollars. Yuma was also picked to be a stopover for the first All-American tour of twenty-five airplanes with 206 support people. In June of 1928 it was announced that the United States meteorological and aerological station would immediately be constructed at Fly Field at a cost of thirty thousand dollars. This station was to be manned by four army personnel.

In 1929, Yuma was selected as first stop for the women's transcontinental air race. Amelia Earhart had problems on landing and nosed her aircraft over, destroying the propeller. A new propeller and mechanics had to be flown in from Los Angeles to repair the aircraft so she could continue in the race. The ladies were not happy with landing in Yuma because their prior stop was in San Bernardino and the next stop for the night was in Phoenix, only a short flight from Yuma. The city had to pay a significant amount to get the racers to stop in Yuma.

PREPARING FOR WORLD WAR II

Development of Fly Field and of aviation in general was slowed due to the Depression, so activity at Fly Field was relatively slow until 1940. It became obvious that the United States was going to be involved in a world war. Part of the ramp-up to war status involved government-sponsored civilian pilot-training programs and the build-up of facilities capable of warfare. Production of warplanes started increasing. In fact it was reported on August 1, 1941, that 11,647 warplanes had been built in the previous year. The War Department needed facilities for training combat pilots and crews. Planning for the Yuma area started as early as 1939 when an aerial tour was made of a potential bombing (aerial gunnery) range to be located between Yuma and Gila Bend, south of U.S. 80. The government didn't make the announcement of this range until September 10, 1941, at which time the Yuma County supervisors recommended that the army consider Fly Field as an army air corps base. Money for the expansion of Fly Field as an emergency defense measure started pouring in early in 1941. This was the start of the takeover of Fly Field under a pending emergency situation. The Yuma newspaper reported on April 23 that funding totaling $781,000 was received for immediate expenditure. The Civil Aeronautics Administration (CAA) provided $151,000; $420,000 was provided under the Work Project Authority (WPA); and $210,000 came through the Federal Priority Board. In August 1941, another $635,000 was made available for repaving the north-south runway and taxiway.

VOLUNTEERS SCAN THE SKIES FOR AERIAL INVADERS

It was also in April 1941 that General George Marshall announced that five hundred thousand civilians would be enrolled as volunteer observers to warn against aerial invaders. Yuma volunteers, under the control of the Fourth Interceptor Command in Riverside, California, lined up to man the aerial observation post located on the water tower at Prison Hill. Their job was to spot and report all aircraft flying in the Yuma area. The major concern was enemy aircraft flying up from Mexico. In May of 1941, a plan for an Office of Civil Defense was announced, and the first order of business was a call for volunteers. The office officially opened for business on December 22, 1941. One group of people formed a local glider club as an important part of national defense. Dick Haile, Leonard Jones, Charly Vomocil, and Nick Wavers started building a BG-7 glider for training purposes.

YUMA COUNTY SHERIFF FORMS AIR PATROL, EVENTUALLY BECOMING A PART OF THE CIVIL AIR PATROL

Sheriff Pete Newman, in November 1941, formed the Sheriff's Air Patrol for the following purposes: to assist in locating lost airplanes and in the event of war to maintain control of power plants and lines, dams, and bridges. This was billed as the most advanced step in law enforcement since the installation of two-way radios in Yuma County, and it eventually became a part of the Civil Air Patrol. The following were appointed to the patrol: Capt. Shields H. Craft, Lt. Denny Wraske, Lt. Ralph Dusenberry, Jerry Nunnaly, Alfred T. Morgan, Kaleel Mittry, J. E. Thomkins, Mrs. D. Wraske, and eighteen-year-old Ty Hemperly. Shortly after this group was formed, Carl Knier, airport manager of the Phoenix Sky Harbor Airport, was appointed wing commander of the Home Defense Aviation Air Patrol. Capt. Craft wrote a letter to Knier offering services of the fully organized Sheriff's Air Patrol. Thus the Yuma group theoretically became the first squadron of the Civil Air Patrol in Arizona.

CIVILIAN AIRCRAFT BANNED FROM FLYING WITHIN 150 MILES OF PACIFIC COAST

It wasn't long after war was declared that civilian aircraft were banned from flying within 150 miles of the Pacific Coast. Fly Field fell just inside the eastern boundary. Therefore, in order for local pilots to keep flying, they moved their aircraft outside of the boundary; most of them moved to Wellton. In February 1942, it was announced that a new airport was being built ten miles east of Yuma, consisting of two runways, 3,000 feet and 2,400 feet long. Shields B. ("Bud") Craft, who had recently been appointed vice commander of the Civil Air Patrol, secured permission and funding from the CAA and the West Coast Command. The airfield was subsequently taken over by the government, which called it Auxiliary One.

Work started at Fly Field in 1941 and was completed in January 1942. Two paved runways, 4,200 feet by 150 feet, were completed. Yuma County had to maintain the field, which was to be used exclusively by army and navy aircraft, since local aircraft were grounded. In June 1942 the War Department announced authorization to spend three million dollars for the army to construct an army air corps training school at Yuma. In July 1942 Capt. Barry M. Goldwater announced to a group of Yuma businessmen that the army air base at Yuma would be one of the largest in the nation and that within a year there would be a force of troops and civilian technicians numbering several thousand. In July 1942 Del E. Webb Company of Phoenix was awarded the contract for construction of the training school. In December 1942 the aerial gunnery range opened east of Yuma and south of U.S. 80. The first class of cadets arrived in January, 1943.

The *City of Yuma* flying north over Fly Field, now called MCAS Yuma and Yuma International Airport.

A BIG VOID CREATED AFTER THE WAR WAS OVER

After the war was over, Yuma Army Air Field (YAAF) was scaled back, and it was declared surplus in September 1946. The Fly Field portion went back under the control of the county, which again called it Fly Field. The government maintained control of the military (south) side; however, local people utilized facilities such as hangars. A few temporary buildings were moved to the civilian (north) side and used as a terminal for a number of years. In 1946, a number of airports (Marsh Downtown, Sturdivant's Somerton, Spain, and Mellon's Yuma Air Park) were established as training schools to take advantage of training pilots under the GI Bill. These airports offered competition to Fly Field, so there was not a lot of activity there.

This changed in April 1949 when the *City of Yuma* endurance flights started using Fly Field as a refueling site. The aircraft was refueled from a Buick convertible driving down the runway with the aircraft flying in formation. This feat was successfully carried out more than 1,500 times without mishap. The objective of the endurance flights was to call attention to the excellent flying weather in Yuma. Three attempts were made by pilots Bob Woodhouse and Woody Jongeward to break the record of 1,008 continuous hours in the air. They managed to break the record and surpass it by 116 hours, thus setting the new record of 1,124 hours. This promotion, which involved over six hundred volunteers, not only succeeded in setting a new record but also received publicity all over the world. This was undoubtedly the most successful promotion with far-reaching results ever carried out in the state of Arizona.

In late 1950 the air force started finalizing plans to reuse the air base. In February the county supervisors entertained a plan to lease the county airfield as a civilian-operated military training base.

Later, the air force sent in two different teams (the final one on May 4, 1951) from Washington and the Western Area Defense Force to conduct a survey to possibly reopen the base on a limited basis. It was only ten days later that Senator Ernest W. McFarland and Congressman Harold A. Patten announced that Yuma Army Air Field would be reactivated. Their announcement went on to say that the chief of engineers would acquire necessary facilities at Yuma County Airport for use as a staging base for gunnery training in connection with Air Defense Operations. This activity would not disrupt civilian flying. A right of entry was given to the U. S. Air Force in June 1951 by the Yuma County Board of Supervisors to lands and certain buildings under their control.

The base was named Vincent Air Force Base in 1956. The air force transferred the air base to the Marine Corps on January 1, 1959. Eventually the civilian side was renamed Yuma International Airport.

CHAPTER TWO

TWO MEN ENDURING FORTY-SEVEN DAYS IN THE AIR

It started as an innocent challenge and through sheer determination and pure tenacity, it developed into one of the greatest and most successful promotions ever conducted in the state of Arizona.

POST-WORLD WAR II DECLINE

The year was 1949, and the place was Yuma, Arizona. Like most cities in the state, Yuma was in the middle of the post-World War II decline. The town's industrial base dwindled drastically after the war with the closing of the large army air base and the other army facilities associated with desert training. The Army Corps of Engineers maintained its Yuma Test Branch (YTB) at Imperial Dam on a reduced scale; but on January 22, 1949, the Corps' prime test area, the Gila desilting basin floor, failed due to high water flow. This failure immediately caused workload effort to diminish. YTB was subsequently closed in January 1950 due to a rift between the Army Corps of Engineers and the Bureau of Reclamation as to fault.

Construction was relatively weak in that only a few housing divisions had been built since the end of the war. That left agriculture as the prime industry with the bureau coming in a distant second. Yuma was not a destination for tourism because not many people outside the state of Arizona had ever heard of Yuma. The Yuma Junior Chamber of Commerce (Jaycees) started holding a world-class rodeo in 1946 that was listed as one of the top ten in the nation, but that news was reaching only a limited number of people. Agriculture was a rising star, thanks to the bureau's lower Colorado Yuma projects. These projects were gradually converting raw desert ground into fertile agricultural land. This highly productive acreage located in the Yuma, Gila, and Dome Valleys and in the Wellton area and the Mohawk Valley to the east had the potential to grow just about any crop, including produce, as long as water continued to flow in the Colorado River.

This lack of a solid, diversified industrial base was a major concern to Yuma businessmen; and as a result, they were keyed to finding ways to broaden this base in order to help Yuma prosper. Individually and in concert with their business organizations, they turned over many stones to try and promote Yuma assets, such as sunshine, unrestricted visibility, and clear skies—with limited success. Try as they might, nobody had yet come up with a successful idea for how to knock a promotional home run. This was about to change.

An Idea Is Born

In late January 1949, members of the Yuma and Parker Chambers of Commerce held a meeting in Parker, about 125 miles north of Yuma. A number of Yuma members attended this meeting. By luck, four local businessmen, Horace "Griff" Griffen, Woody Jongeward, Ray Smucker, and F. C. "Frosty" Braden, traveled together in one car. After they arrived in Parker, Glen Strohm, a Parker businessman whom they all knew, joined them for a tour of the town, since this was one of the scheduled activities. During the tour, the conversation turned to two adventurous pilots in California, who were attempting to break the world record for keeping a single-engine aircraft flying continuously for an extended period of time. Glen, Woody, and Griff had previously known one of the pilots, Bill Barris, whom they had met during the government's civilian pilot training (CPT) prior to World War II. Bill and his partner, Dick Riedel, were flying an Aeronca Sedan AC-15 known as the *Sunkist Lady* out of Fullerton, California, in their effort to surpass the world endurance flight record of 726 hours. The Yuma men noted that these two pilots were getting a lot of attention from radio and the newspapers.

Ray Smucker, who was known for his quick promotional mind and who was manager of Yuma's only radio station, KYUM, spoke up, "You know, there is a lot of publicity in an endurance flight. We could have one in Yuma. We'd show the world that we have 365 flying days a year and get our air base reactivated." The seed was planted and ready to be watered.

Horace Griffen recalls that the gist of the conversation the rest of the day was just kidding about it. The word had spread quickly among the other Yuma delegates, and they all had their opinions on the subject. Later, on the way back to Yuma, the subject came up again, and Woody, normally a man of few words, stated in no uncertain terms, "Okay, Ray, you get the airplane, and Griff and I will fly it!"

The challenge was made and the spotlight was focused on Ray.

Within three days of that first conversation in the car, Horace Griffen received a call from Ray Smucker. "Well, Griff, I've found an airplane, and we're having a kick-off meeting at Pete Byrne's office today at noon." Pete Byrne was an attorney in Yuma, and the men realized that a legal mind would be needed.

Ray Smucker was a man full of creative ideas. He initiated numerous programs to benefit young people and others in his town, and the city named Smucker Park after him. He had a half-hour radio program on KYUM every morning called *The Sunny Side of the Street*. As people drove to work, they heard him expressing sympathy for his unfortunate old friends back in "North Overshoe, Iowa." He said that the only problem faced by Yumans was "Where can we go for our health?"

He was president of the Arizona Junior Chamber of Commerce and suggested that the Yuma Jaycees sponsor the endurance flight project. That was their head coach talking, and to say that they ran with that ball and scored would be an understatement.

Horace Griffen owned a Buick dealership, which required his attention to the extent that he declined the honor (or the task) of being one of the pilots. The still-small group of planners determined that Bob Woodhouse was a likely candidate to fly with Woody. Bob was parts manager at Griffen Buick and, like Woody, a former navy pilot. He loved to fly almost more than he loved to eat. He accepted the responsibility after Horace agreed to continue his salary.

Woody owned an electrical repair business with his brother, Howard, who agreed to keep the business going. Woody was thirty-one years old and Bob was twenty-six. Both were married. One can only imagine the reactions of Betty Jongeward and Berta Woodhouse to this "crazy idea."

As the meetings continued happening and growing in size in Pete Byrne's office, many people reacted initially with some shock and amazement. Their questions about the logistics of accomplishing such an incredible feat were quickly answered by those who had been thinking about it for a few days. The group of volunteers multiplied rapidly as businesses and individuals offered their support and their almost-endless hours of work.

THE PLAN DEVELOPS

The airplane, loaned generously by Claude Sharpensteen and Mickey Lorang of the AA Amusement Company, was an Aeronca Sedan AC-15, N1156H, a four-place airplane with a 145-horsepower Continental engine. Marsh Aviation made its hangar facilities at the downtown airport available along with its head mechanic, Paul Burch, who was considered the maestro of aeronautics in Yuma. He, Bill Wilcox, Dallas Hovatter, and Eddie Mendivil quickly went to work modifying the airplane. The right front seat and the backseat were removed. Auxiliary fuel tanks were installed, as the original wing tanks held only thirty-six gallons of usable fuel. Two tanks, with associated hoses and pumps, were installed in the fuselage, one vertical and one horizontal in the baggage area. They took up the entire baggage compartment and a portion of the rear seat area.

A view showing the two fuselage tanks, one horizontal and one vertical, with the rotary pump used to transfer fuel from the two-and-one-half-gallon cream cans into these tanks. Later, the same pump is used to transfer the gasoline from these tanks up to the wing tanks.

A view, looking forward on the co-pilot's side, showing the big pot that allowed for the addition and extraction of oil to and from the crankcase. This allowed the pilots to change the oil every one hundred hours.

The off-duty pilot used a hand-operated rotary pump to transfer fuel from the two and-one-half-gallon cream cans into the fuselage tanks and later into the wing tanks. The addition of those tanks increased the total usable fuel capacity from thirty-six to over eighty gallons. Another system was designed and installed that allowed monitoring of oil quantity in the engine crankcase and a means to add and extract oil from the crankcase, thus, making oil changes available. Dallas Hovatter built a door that folded up and was fastened open, up and out of the way when necessary.

The plan was that the pilots would take turns at the controls in four-hour shifts. During the time that each man was not on duty as pilot, he could sleep, do physical exercises, and take care of the various chores that needed to be done to keep the mission on track.

The refueling car, a 1948 Buick Super convertible provided by Griffen Buick, had belonged to George Murdock, Griff's service manager, who married author Shirley Woodhouse, Bob's younger sister, just two years after the endurance flight. George and Bob had initially practiced some refueling procedures with George in his Buick and Bob in George's Taylorcraft. That airplane held only two passengers; it was too small to be used for the flight and too lightweight to fly in formation with a speeding car. As the plans for the flight progressed, Griff and George made a deal involving George trading in that 1948 Buick convertible for a 1949 Buick Sedanette. Charlie Gilpin and Charlie Worthen of Bert's Welding Works, which was owned by Bert Parrish, built a platform in the backseat area of the convertible with a protective railing around it. That platform provided a safe place for members of the refueling crew to stand when the car was speeding down the runway and they were handing food, fuel, and other supplies to the pilots.

Union Oil Company came into the picture as a major sponsor. They provided all of the gasoline and oil for the airplane throughout the project. The aviation gasoline was stored at Marsh's downtown airport where Bert Coffee filled the individual cans, filtering the gasoline through a chamois skin to remove any lint or other foreign matter. Then Chuck Mabery and Keith Smith ("Smitty") transported the full cans to the county airport in a truck provided by Union Oil Company through Norman Bann, the local distributor. Some members of the refueling crew then transferred a few cans to the Buick convertible at the beginning of each refueling run.

DETAILED OPERATIONAL PLAN MATERIALIZES

The driver of the Buick accelerated rapidly to a speed of about sixty-five to seventy miles an hour down a runway or across the triangular air base in whatever direction was into the wind. The entire paved air base was theirs to be used as needed. There was no military activity and very little commercial operation on the base; it belonged to Yuma County. Constant radio communication was maintained between the airplane and the Buick by virtue of the expertise of Paul Estep, a radio specialist with the Civil Aeronautics Authority. Charlie Weeks was a radioman in the navy and worked for AA Amusement Company, and he also worked on the radios during the flight.

Woody and Betty Jongeward and Bob and Berta Woodhouse at Marsh Airport prior
to takeoff.

Pilots Woody Jongeward and Bob Woodhouse with the *City of Yuma* at Marsh
Airport just before flight.

Official start of record-breaking flight at Marsh Airport, Yuma. Roy Slaten, manager of Western Union in Yuma, serves as timer. Observers are, left to right, Ethelind Woodhouse (Bob's mother), Berta Woodhouse, and Betty Jongeward.

Showing layout of controls and instruments that were added, including radio.

The Aeronca, dubbed the *City of Yuma* and emblazoned with that name and the slogan "The City With a Future, Yuma, 365 Flying Days Yearly," then joined up on the speeding convertible. The pilot maintained an altitude of only a few feet so that supplies could be handed up swiftly but carefully by the intrepid ground crew to the copilot of the moment. Both pilot and driver had to maintain a strictly businesslike attitude, dissuaded by nothing, eyes straight ahead, speeds synchronized exactly in an unchanging direction. They conducted a smooth relationship until the driver yelled "Geronimo" and the crew members sat down and braced themselves while the driver applied brakes with great determination to get that Buick stopped before it ran off the end of the five-thousand-foot runway into the soft, sandy desert. The pilot had possible wind gusts to consider, knowing that his right wheel was near the spotlight of the Buick. It was also close to the head of his long-time friend who was driving the car. The right hubcap of the airplane sustained several dents from bumping the spotlight during the flight, and the spotlight had to be replaced twice.

The off-duty pilot leaned out of the open door and down in order to grab the handle of the can filled with lifeblood for the Aeronca and bring it aboard. He was supported by a specially-devised safety belt which enabled him to use both hands to pick up the fuel cans. He then placed each can in the backseat area as quickly as possible, almost at the same moment that he reached for another, or for cans of oil, their meals, water for bathing and shaving, clean towels, or changes of clothing. At times, even a high-speed kiss was exchanged between co-pilot and wife, as she stood tall in the Buick, supported or even boosted up by the versatile members of the refueling crew. Usually there were about twelve runs for fuel and one for food, clothing, and other supplies.

Early morning refueling, on first attempt, with Woody flying, Griff driving the refueling car, Berta riding along as passenger, and Bob Hodge handing breakfast and lunch to Bob. Photo by Sammy Watkins.

Another view of refueling with airplane higher, showing the upper limit of this action, with cans being passed down. Grounding rod not used after first two attempts, as it was determined that this was not needed.

During a normal single pass down the runway, four cans of gasoline were usually handed up to the pilots. At the end of the runway, the two vehicles broke formation and the copilot transferred the newly acquired gasoline into the fuselage tanks by using the hand-operated rotary pump as the pilot circled and prepared to join up on the car for another pass down the runway. They were then able to hand down empty cans as well as take on full ones in subsequent runs. There were over 1,500 such passes made by the time the endurance flight ended.

Congestion of cabin is evident. Note how wing strut is wrapped with rope as protection during fuel transfer. Also, the Plexiglass layer protects fuselage fabric. Note marks on Plexiglass.

Two refueling crews were used. Originally there were two refueling events each day. One was at 6:00 A.M. and the other at 6:00 P.M. Horace Griffen drove the Buick for the morning refueling with Bernie Pensky, Chuck Mabery, Keith Smith, and Howard Jongeward as the rest of the crew. In the evening, Charlie Gilpin drove the car with Bob Hodge, Norm Bann, Louie Mueller, and Ralph Michaels handling the gasoline cans. Phil Neese was on "stand by." Betty Jongeward and Berta Woodhouse were always on hand, taking turns riding in the refueling car. Bill Linder, Floyd Estes, and Russell Phillips served regularly in various capacities.

"There was no committee chairman who assigned tasks, saying, 'You will do this. Or, can you do that? It all just fell into place,'" Griff mentioned.

Horace Griffen made available his service department, including George Murdock, his service manager. In addition to his duties at Griffen Buick, George was also tasked to keep the Buick in top running condition. Since cars of that day were not as reliable as today's, this was almost a full-time job, especially toward the latter weeks of the flight. Due to the nature of how the car was being used, several sets of tires and front brake assemblies had to be installed to keep it safe. In those days, you couldn't get more than ten thousand miles out of a set of tires under normal driving conditions. Today, it is not unusual to get up to seventy thousand miles. Fortunately for George, Goodyear Tire Company eventually took over the tire-changing responsibilities and donated "a couple of sets of tires," as he remembers. Harold Sturges was manager of the Goodyear store. However, George had to handle all other aspects of keeping the car going. He had to take care of all driver complaints in addition to keeping the car tuned to perfection. He had to tune the car twice a week, including changing the points and spark plugs. One day Griff said that the car was just not accelerating as well as it normally did. After running a series of tests to determine the cause, George decided to change the engine. In those days, Buick issued engines to dealers that were complete with all accessories. The engine would run in the box if you added a battery and fuel. This allowed George to be able to change out the engine overnight. He completed it at about 3:30 A.M., in time for the early morning refueling. That was another little drama within the bigger story.

Griffen Buick also provided a GMC pickup to run alongside the refueling car for photographers and other observers. Almost all of the newsreels and professional photographs were taken from that pickup during refuelings. Emil Eger, Sammy Watkins, and Art Fszol were local professional photographers who took dozens of excellent photos. Amateur photographer Charly Vomocil took Kodak color slides, which were the only color photos taken.

Refueling car with Spud Parker, Bob Hodge, Charlie Gilpin, Paul Burch, and Louis Mueller. Photo by Rod Daley.

The 4:00 A.M. refueling crew: Griff (the driver), Bernie Pensky, Chuck Mabery, and Keith ("Smitty") Smith. Also shown are the two-and-one-half-gallon cream cans used for transferring fuel. Photo by Emil Eger.

OTHER SPONSORS START LINING UP

Major sponsors of this venture were the Yuma Jaycees; AA Amusement Company; Griffen Buick; Jongeward Electric; Penn Signs; Marsh Aviation; Goodyear Tire Company; and Union Oil Company, which provided approximately nine thousand gallons of aviation gasoline and two hundred quarts of oil used; Continental Engines, which replaced the engine after the flight; and Tate and Hobart, the Shell Oil distributor, which provided the gasoline and oil for the refueling car—no small matter. The entire city got involved: restaurants, a laundry, a sign company, a welding shop, service stations, petroleum distributors, and a long list of about seventy businesses donated support. Meals were prepared by the Valley Café, a popular local restaurant managed by Whitey Stanton. They were picked up and delivered to the refueling crew by Harold Breech, chief of police; Jim Birmingham and Bert Power, police sergeants; and Ray Prather. Dr. Ralph T. Irwin was the official physician for the pilots. He wrote up their diet, which was low in fat, salt, and calories, with some other restrictions. Both men lost several pounds during the flight. Woody weighed 133 pounds at the beginning of the flight, and he lost thirteen of them. Bob weighed in at 137, and he lost eight pounds. They had no real problem with that; they spent a lot of time with their feet under dinner tables after the flight was over.

The slogan for the flight of the *City of Yuma* was "Ten-Ten!" Since the existing record set by Barris and Riedel was 1,008 hours, the Jaycees established 1,010 hours as a minimum goal and "Ten-Ten!" was the radio call signal for the refueling car.

FIRST AND SECOND ATTEMPTS FAIL

Because of mechanical problems, the pilots had to give up and land twice without accomplishing their goal. The first attempt began on April 21, 1949, at 4:51:50 P.M. and lasted only seventy-four hours.

Bob described what happened: "During the evening refueling run, the engine began to lose power, runnin' on five cylinders. We were just goin' out from the airport after a run, and Woody was flyin' that time, and this thing is quiverin' and shakin' and backfirin'—one thing and another—and so we make a turn back, like you're not supposed to do, you know, but there are orange trees out there the way we were goin', and so it's better to get back to the airport if you can. If we'd had to land in those orange trees, we could have done that anywhere, but it would have damaged the airplane. Anyway, we got back to the airport and landed after a short conversation with Paul

Burch. We decided to land and correct the problem before serious damage could occur to the engine. Then Paul and Bill Wilcox found the problem, and it took a couple of weeks to repair and then we started again." They found that the original wing tank vents were not adequate for this method of refueling, which caused a vapor lock. This, in turn, caused the engine to overheat, burning a valve in one cylinder.

Bob and Woody flew to Fullerton, California, in another airplane, to attend the landing of Barris and Riedel's airplane upon completion of *their* record-breaking flight. Bob's parents, Harold and Ethelind Woodhouse, flew to that event also in their own Cessna.

The second attempt of the Yuma pilots to break the world endurance flight record began on May 5, 1949, at 7:51 A.M. The pilots were forced to land again on May 12 after only 155 hours and 17 minutes in the air.

"That time," Bob said, "we started havin' a detonation problem again. I was flyin' it at the moment, and we had it on a high-power setting and, as we're goin' out, climbin' out, very slowly. The thing starts quiverin' and shakin', and so I just started to turn—we were barely at the edge of the airport, and I started to turn back around—of course, there was nothin' goin' on at the airport, you know, it's just about five hundred acres of blacktop, and I'm tryin' to switch tanks, do anything, you can't do very much, you know, for an airplane like that. If it's gettin' fuel, it runs, and if it doesn't, it doesn't. So, anyway, we made a trip around the airport, about ten feet high, in about a fifteen-degree bank, pullin' carburetor heat and checkin' the mixture control and one thing and another. Nothin' did any good, but about the time we started the second lap around the airport, we were flyin' in a trail of smoke, and, you know, it's pretty obvious where that came from. And about that time, there was a big explosion, and it blew the crankshaft oil seal out of the front end of the engine and against the propeller. When you get a hole in the piston, then you build up too much crankcase pressure; then you've got a volatile mixture in there, and so it wasn't too hard to figure out that it was all over right there. The windshield was all covered with oil. This was a problem that was insurmountable, and we just rolled the thing level and landed. We all began to think about Smucker after that, how he got us into this deal. He was the perpetrator, for sure.

"The airplane had to go through a modification process, and in the meantime, Continental Motors had come out with a different crankshaft, a much better one, so the Jaycees bought that (and I think they were in debt up to their ears) but we got the thing ready to fly."

At the fortieth-anniversary party, Woody said, "An interesting thing about the flight we did: one of the difficult things was cooling the engine. First of all, Paul Burch had rebuilt the engine, and he put more clearance; he put a few thousandths more clearance between the pistons and the shoulder wall to make it run cooler—and he was right. It worked. He also put some extra scoops out in front to make it scoop more air at low speed so as to cool it down. And it was a hot year. Our problem was to get to altitude without overheating the engine. We had thermocouples in all the cylinders and a read-out gauge and monitors. After a refueling, we'd slowly get up to about eight thousand feet where it was cool and wait till it was time to refuel again. It was kind of a chore getting that done. I think that was one of the more interesting things about the flight. You think about the refueling runs being the most dramatic part of the flight; but actually, nursing that airplane up and down was a good share of it also. We did enjoy getting up to altitude. It's about twenty-five to thirty degrees cooler at eight thousand feet—and we were able to get up there where the air was clean and fresh. Besides, the guys in the refueling crews were passing a lot of gas."

It took months to get some of the parts needed. One of the modifications was the installation of a sight gauge to show the amount of oil in the crankcase.

The pilots, refueling crews, mechanics, and all of the city of Yuma were undaunted and eager to launch another effort.

The Third Attempt

The endurance fliers finally took off for their third attempt at the world record at 7:15:50 P.M. on August 24, 1949. Roy Slaten, manager of Western Union, was the official timer. Those wheels never touched the ground again until October 10—1,124 hours, 14 minutes and 5 seconds, almost forty-seven days later.

When the endurance fliers were just past the halfway mark toward breaking the record, on their twenty-second day in the air, a third refueling was initiated. An article in the *Yuma Daily Sun* explained: "At noon today, the ex-Navy pilots passed their 545th hour of continuous flying as they winged onward toward their goal of 1010 hours. Now more than halfway through the proposed record-breaking flight, the pilots and crews are taking extra precautions to lessen the chances of anything marring a heretofore perfect performance.

"In an effort to keep the plane's load as light as possible, the refueling operations will be strung out over a longer length of time. This morning, the refuelers started the operation a couple of hours early, dragging out at 4:00 instead of the usual 6:00. The darkness automatically slowed down the operation.

"Yuma Jaycees said today that they want to chill many rumors around town that the plane is having difficulty. The change in refueling schedule is more of a preventive move than a curative measure."

The time span through the night was thus divided up during the last three weeks of the flight. The runs for the 4:00 A.M. refueling, in total darkness, added another dramatic element. That heightened the interest and the concern around town. At that early hour, the pilots took on only enough fuel to last them until "the regular morning show," usually making three passes for fuel and one for breakfast and toilet articles. Horace Griffen drove the car for that refueling as well as the regular morning run, which was then changed from 6:00 A.M. to 8:00 A.M.

Even before the predawn refueling was adopted, flare pots and lamps were kept burning along one runway every night. They had to be cleaned, filled, and lighted each evening in case of a nighttime emergency landing. Paul Burch's daughter, Shirley, says that some people have mentioned to her that they remember doing that task when they were in high school.

Bob explained to a group of interested Yumans how the pilots first got "in tune" with the Buick for those passes. "Well," he said, "as the pilot, you're lookin' straight ahead, and you're seein' stuff out of your peripheral vision. We got where we could feel, when we'd start lettin' down to join up on the car, the right wing would get into some air that's comin' over the top of the car, so you'd have to roll a little right aileron into it to push that wing down. All of a sudden, it's flyin' in air that's not comin' straight to it, so you've got more lift. Well, you get a little deeper down in there, then some of that air that's comin' off the side of the car begins hittin' the tail, so you have to hold left rudder and right aileron. It's a cross-control situation. But then, as you go down into that disturbed air, you get into just the right position, which would be about when the right wheel is level with the spotlight on the Buick, then that sensation begins to go away, because that air is gettin' high enough above you. You could actually feel that, without lookin', you could feel that."

In describing how they learned the exact altitude to fly when joining up with the refueling car, Bob explained, "When Woody was flyin', I'd put my hand up by the top of the instrument panel where he could see it. I told him, 'Just do what you're doin' regardin' altitude, and if you're too high, I'll point down, and you can work your way down; if you're too low, I'll signal up.' So that's how we worked out that business of gettin' in the right position with the car."

He said, "It all went together very well. When we started out plannin' all this, we were gonna pick up those gas cans on a rope. Charlie Gilpin made a deal for us, out of a steel shaft about six feet long, that had a hook on one end of it, and we had a cable on top of these gas cans, and we were just gonna snap that into that hook, and we'd pull the can up. Well, we got out there to practice with a can of water, and Woody was flyin', and Griff was chasin' this shaft around that probably weighed about ten pounds or more, on the end of about twenty-five feet of rope, and you can imagine what that thing was doin' down there in that disturbed air from the airplane. So we picked up a can, and it took almost a mile to do it. When I started pickin' that can up, it was pullin' the airplane down, so the can dragged along the runway, and the bottom was torn out of it. So I just threw the whole thing away, and I said, 'Woody, we're gonna get this stuff by hand. It may take a while.'"

Many people volunteered an incredible amount of time and energy and the refueling crew members' jobs were dangerous, but not one of them hesitated. It was considered an honor to serve on one of the refueling crews.

Griff says, "Our daughter, Judy, was born at 2:00 in the afternoon on September 12, and I was present for her birth, but I didn't miss a refueling run."

ENGINE PROBLEMS DEVELOP

"About the only problems that we had on the third flight," Bob remembered, "were [*sic*] the engine began to run rough after about three or four weeks. We called Paul Burch, and he called the technician for Union Oil Company, Paul Goodwin, and he was in Alaska. He had an SNJ airplane that he used for transportation, and he beat it right down here. I think Paul came up with the idea. He sent us up a pint jar of water and a roll of maskin' tape and a couple of wrenches. He told us to take the vacuum line off the back of the manifold pressure gauge, put a piece of maskin' tape over that line, and punch a pinhole in it, and then put it in this pint of water. That causes some water vapor goin' into the engine. It was carbon buildup, is what it was. We did all of that, accordin' to Paul's instructions. Griff was flyin' along under us in a Navion, and he started seein' stuff come out—smoke and stuff—and then it started runnin' clean, runnin' better, so we put the line back on the gauge and went ahead."

The pilots and refueling crews had almost no trouble with the weather. Charlie Gilpin, president of the Junior Chamber of Commerce, said that they had about three drops of rain one evening shortly before they landed and that they experienced about twenty-two minutes of a wind storm one day. The *Sun* quoted the pilots as saying that every day was, "as we used to say in the navy, the kind of a day when we wondered why anybody would want to stay on the ground."

Bob said, "There was one time, however, when a dirt storm came up in the afternoon. We could see it comin' when it was down south of Mexicali. So we got on the radio, and the car had a radio in it, and we called the guys, and they rounded up the crew that filled the gas cans, and they all came hustlin' out to the airport. By that time, the storm was right down this side of Somerton. It was a big wall of dirt. We used the diagonal runway because that's the way the wind was that afternoon, and we made about two or three passes, and the dirt was almost gettin' to us. The turbulent air that was ahead of the dirt had got there. We hit a pretty violent little whirly thing, and, if you'll notice, on the right-hand strut, it's wrapped with rope. There's a hunk of manila rope wrapped around the strut. Paul Burch had anticipated that if the strut ever came in contact with the pipe on the refueling car, the strut could be bent, and it might reduce its integrity and weaken the airplane, so he had wrapped that rope around it for a ways. It was a bumper, and we did bump it a pretty good lick that evening, and it didn't hurt it.

"But then, we got out of there and headed out east and slowly climbed away from it all. We'd taken enough gas to last us until the storm was over, and then we came back and did the evening refueling before dark."

THE WHOLE TOWN IS INTO IT

There were many people in town who flashed their yard lights on and off, thinking that "the boys up there" were responding to them because the pilots also blinked their lights on and off. In fact, Bob and Woody were communicating in Morse code with their friends, including Chuck and Smitty, who were sitting in Betty's yard, having beer and a "conversation" using a flashlight. Finally, there were so many yard lights flashing, that the pilots had to give up trying to locate their earthbound communicants.

One day Smucker suggested in his morning radio program, *The Sunny Side of the Street,* that everybody take a white tea towel (or diaper or something white) to wave at the pilots when they came around for their refueling runs that evening. The *Yuma Daily Sun* featured a picture of that activity the next day. It was just one more way for the people in the crowd to show their enthusiasm.

Evening refueling. The crowd is waving tea towels (or diapers)—another way of showing enthusiasm and support.

For the last three weeks of the flight, the Arizona network of radio stations broadcast a live interview with the pilots every morning. After the 8:00 A.M. refueling, the Buick was driven to KYUM where Ray Smucker, using the radio in the refueling car, talked things over with Bob and Woody and sent the conversations out over Arizona.

As they approached the existing world endurance flight record, they were in the national news regularly. KYUM was affiliated with NBC, and Morgan Beatty, on his *News of the World* program, mentioned the "Yuma, Arizona, Endurance Flight" every evening at five o'clock, after the former record was broken. He would say something like, "Let's see if those boys are still in the air, so now we'll switch to KYUM, the hottest little station in the nation."

Ray Smucker said, "We then brought in one of the pilots on the radio, so every night, either Bob or Woody talked on the radio, nationwide, and reported on how things were going." A clipping service sent articles from thirty-two foreign countries, and they received letters from Germany, the Philippines, and Japan.

1916 Buick ("alternate chase car"), Horace Griffen (driving), George Murdock (passenger with "grounding rod"), Bernie Pensky (in backseat), Paul Dawson of KYUM radio station (on microphone). Others not identified.

When they broke the record, the town went "bananas." The magic moment was at 7:15:50 P.M. on October 5. The entire city went dark for one minute prior to that time by virtue of a master switch at the main power source for the streetlights and residential lights. Then, at the appropriate second, the fire department whistle gave three short blasts. Factory and train whistles; police, ambulance, and fire truck sirens; and thousands of automobile horns sounded. Yuma made itself heard, and the lights came on again.

The Beginning of the End

Near the end of the flight, the pilots and the airplane were becoming increasingly fatigued. The nighttime refuelings were a source of some concern, but they continued to be accomplished successfully. The pilots had planned to land on Columbus Day, but their plans changed. On October 9 they flew over to Los Alamitos Naval Air Station in Southern California, where they took part in a "fly-over" as the opening event of an air show. The navy had sent some officers over to Yuma to invite them to do that. Both Bob and Woody were in the navy reserves, and the navy's Blue Angels were participating in the show. Their friends, Barris and Riedel, former endurance flight record holders, were there as part of that show also. Horace Griffen, Betty Jongeward, and Berta Woodhouse flew to Los Alamitos for that occasion, where they were treated like visiting dignitaries.

"Well," Bob later admitted, "the night before we went over there, we were gonna have a morning refueling, and then fly over to Los Alamitos. Well, about midnight that night, we checked somethin' that we did every hour; we checked all the cylinders. We had magneto switches, you know. So, on one mag, the thing was runnin' kinda rough. It's supposed to run on both mags, and it was fine on both, and it was fine on the left one; but on the right one, it was kinda quiverin' and missin'.

"So, when I woke Woody up to take over at the end of my four-hour shift, I told him, 'I want you to listen to somethin'.' So we did that check, and it was shakin' on that one mag, but on both it was still pretty good.

"Woody said, 'What are we gonna do about that?'

"I said, 'Well, we aren't gonna check the mags any more till we get back from Los Alamitos!'

"Then coming back out here over the sand dunes, we switched to that mag, and it just quit completely. Of course, the prop continued to windmill, which sort of loaded the exhaust system up with unburned fuel, and then, when we turned it back on, we got a big explosion. A big flash of fire came out of the exhaust stack. The bottom of the wing was polished aluminum, so it lit things up pretty well. Anyway, when we got back to the air base, we told the refueling crew that we had something that we wanted them to listen to. Then we did that trick for them.

"Paul Burch came up with an idea real quick as a remedy for that. He was gonna send us up a magneto and some wrenches and a hack saw and 'Let's see, we gotta have some tin snips.' The plan was—and it wouldn't have been impossible to do this—if we wanted to continue, we would take the tin snips, cut a hole in the firewall, and then we would take all the wires off the magneto and set them aside. The magneto was bolted on with two nuts, so we'd take one nut off, and then we were gonna go to about thirteen thousand feet, shut the airplane off, get the prop to completely stop windmillin', and then all we had to do—and we would have had about thirty minutes to do this—well, the hacksaw was because there was a structural member that went across right behind where that magneto was, and you could get it off from the outside, but we were gonna have to cut that piece of the airplane out of there.

"All of that could have been done, but when Paul was tellin' us this, I was lookin' at Woody, and Woody was lookin' at me, and we were thinkin', 'You know, we own this record; what are we tryin' to do?'

"So we voted Paul down. He didn't complain, and neither did anybody else. We said, 'Well, what we're gonna do is this: we'll fly the rest of tonight, and we'll refuel about every hour, a few cans of gas, and keep the airplane light so we don't have to use very much power, and then, anytime, whenever—Smucker was the guy who was the contact man with the media—whatever time he wants this news release thing, that's when we'll land. That was critical, I guess, regardin' the time of day, because of the national media."

LET'S SEE IF WE CAN GET THIS THING ON THE GROUND

The time for the historic landing was set at about 3:15 P.M., and the local schools all closed early so that the busses could take the children to the airport to witness the landing. There were fire trucks, ambulances, a doctor, and police officers standing by all night because the "Old Faithful" engine was running less smoothly during the refuelings.

Crowd, estimated at twelve thousand to fifteen thousand, at landing of the *City of Yuma* after setting the world's record, October 10, 1949.

A portion of the crowd at the landing. Note the *Sunkist Lady,* Aeronca Sedan 15-AC at far left, which held the old record of 1,008 hours. Woman in white shirt near left is Elizabeth Wright, mother of Robert Wright, former Farmers Insurance agent of Yuma. Photo by Rod Daley.

Virtually all businesses in Yuma closed at noon, and officials estimated that the crowd gathered at the airport was between twelve thousand and fifteen thousand people. Those officials said that there were about six thousand cars parked in the vicinity of the airport. When one considers that the total population of the town was only about nine thousand people, the spirit that permeated the entire county becomes evident.

When they were just about to land, Woody said to Horace Griffen on the radio, "Do you know what day this is? It's 'Ten-Ten'—October tenth!" Coincidentally, their landing date played right into that theme, which had originally meant 1,010 hours.

Eight navy F6F Hellcats came over from Los Alamitos and formed an "aerial blanket" as the *City of Yuma* landed.

Bob said, "That was kind of a reciprocal deal for us havin' flown over there. But we had a sick airplane, and those guys in the fighter planes had their flaps down and everything, and they're goin' around the airport, and there was no way we could keep up with them. So we got on the inside of the circle, and they were on the outside, makin' a bigger circle."

Then the military airplanes passed over the airport twice in a spectacular crisscross pattern, and a fireworks display was set off from a nearby hill by the police department. The roar of the crowd is still remembered by the old-timers of Yuma. They were wishing that the pilots could hear them.

Bob said, "We had the guys in the refueling car come along and punch the tires and make sure we didn't have a flat tire, because we might have had a little trouble on landin' if we'd had a flat tire. The tires were pretty soft, and that shows up in the movies. The tires are makin' a kind of wide footprint there."

Bob said, "The time of the landing came on Woody's shift. He was a little worried because we hadn't landed for seven weeks, and we had knocked a spotlight or two off of the side of the Buick and bent the hubcap all up on the airplane. It wasn't really a problem, but we decided that I was gonna look at the ground real hard and tell him if he's three feet high or two feet high or whatever. So when he comes in to land and I'm lookin' at the asphalt, which is goin' by about sixty miles an hour, it's kind of hard to tell just how high you are.

"Woody said, 'How's that?'

"I said, 'It's too high,' so he comes down about a foot, and we made a couple of adjustments like that, and it got down to where it looked pretty good to me, and I told him to go ahead, cut it off, and land it. So he closed the throttle. Well, when he did, he began to feather the nose up a little, and the airplane started fallin'. We had been about three feet high. He said that he heard me say, 'Oh oh!' Well, I wouldn't have done any better."

Before stepping out of the airplane for the first time in almost seven weeks, the endurance fliers taxied around the field so that everyone could get a close-up view and pictures of the *City of Yuma*. The pilots had wondered whether or not they would be able to walk. They were, although somewhat hesitantly at first.

October 10, 1949. Berta and Bob Woodhouse and Woody and Betty Jongeward with congratulatory horseshoe of flowers.

Pilots Bob and Woody shortly after the landing. At right is Bob's mother, Ethelind Woodhouse, also a pilot.

Bill Barris and Dick Riedel, previous record holders, congratulate Bob and Woody.

Pilots and their wives on a celebratory victory ride around the crowd at the airport. Horace Griffen is chauffeur in brand new 1949 Buick convertible.

POST-FLIGHT CELEBRATIONS

There was another celebration on October 12. Pilots, refueling crews, and other volunteers had been able to return to a semblance of their normal lives. The Yuma Union High School band led a parade, and the pilots and their wives sat up on the back of a new Buick convertible. They were presented with a gigantic horseshoe of flowers and were officially honored by their town and their state.

The dateline, "Yuma, Arizona," had shown up on metropolitan front pages and in major magazines and was heard on radios around the world, attracting attention to the 365 days of flying weather and the huge, inactive air base. On the day that the record was broken, the *Chicago Tribune* carried a front-page color photograph and attending article. The *Arizona Republic's* main headline on October 11 was "YUMA ENDURANCE FLIERS LAND," and the subtitles were, "Record Set at 1,124 Air Hours," and "Huge Throng Greets Airmen; Both Appear in Good Condition." At the landing on October 10, newsreel photographers were present along with many reporters and network radio newsmen from near and far.

"The whole world heard about Yuma, Arizona," Ray Smucker said.

The pilots received congratulations from all over the world, but soon life for the major players started returning to normal with the exception of Yuma. As Ray Smucker had predicted, the attention given to Yuma during the flight started paying dividends as Yuma was named one of ten potential sites for the location of the U.S. Air Force Academy. On April 1, 1951, the Yuma Test Branch was reopened as a desert environmental test facility and renamed Yuma Test Station. The air force reactivated the airbase on July 7, 1951, as a training base. Yuma began a population explosion. It was and is, as proclaimed in the slogan on the side of that little airplane, "the city with a future."

It should be pointed out that all of the work toward this project was in the nature of public service. Volunteers did it all. As Horace Griffen and Ray Smucker have often said, "Nobody made a dime in profit from the flight."

CHAPTER THREE

THE *CITY OF YUMA* RISES FROM THE ASHES

The airplane, after being sold in 1953, was subsequently damaged in a ground loop while landing in Kansas. For some unknown reason, in July 1953, someone requested that the CAA cancel the registration due to a crash.

In September 1953, a request was made to the CAA to reinstate the registration, which it did. Many people in Yuma heard about the cancellation of the registration but not the reregistration. The rumor went around for a number of years that 56H had crashed and burned, totally destroying it. Shirley Burch and her sisters, Susie and Sally, grew up helping their father, Paul Burch, work on airplanes. They always pressured their dad to find 56H and bring it back to Yuma and fix it up. Shirley remembers that Paul always said, "The airplane crashed and burned; it doesn't exist anymore." In reality, the damage was fixable, and 56H was returned to service and converted to a floatplane in 1978 when it was owned by Duane Cole. Cole also had a 180 HP Lycoming with a constant-speed prop installed. It went through a series of owners (a total of nineteen). In the meanwhile Woody and Bob were inducted into the Arizona Aviation Hall of Fame, and it became generally known that 56H was alive and well. Gary Oden of McElhaney Cattle Co. in Wellton led the action to get Woody and Bob placed in that Hall of Fame. It was during the time leading up to their induction that Gary asked Bill Cutter of Cutter Aviation in Phoenix to track the airplane down, which he did. The owner was contacted; but the asking price seemed a little high, so no further action was taken.

THE SEARCH BEGINS

Also in 1991, Jim Gillaspie asked a friend, Dick LeMay, to look in the FAA registry to determine who owned 56H. He reported that Charlie Neal of Staples, Minnesota, owned it. Jim's interest was to perhaps buy the airplane, return it to Yuma, restore it to the 1949 configuration, and reintroduce it to the people of Yuma. This plan was never implemented; however, in late October 1996, another friend, Elmer Kettunen, called one day and asked Jim what he thought about bringing 56H back to Yuma. Jim told him that it was an excellent idea and then asked if he wanted to know where it was located. That simple question started another round of togetherness between the people of Yuma and the *City of Yuma*.

Elmer called Charlie Neal to find out if he would sell it. Charlie replied that he had recently lost his medical certificate due to a brain aneurysm and, yes, he would sell the airplane. He said that his son, Chris, flew it at the time, but he owned a crop-dusting service, and he didn't need to fly that airplane. Elmer subsequently called two other people, Horace Griffen and Orval McVey, to join the group. At the first meeting, everybody agreed that they should bring 56H back to Yuma and that Jim should head up the effort since he was the youngest. At a subsequent meeting, Horace Griffen reported that he had talked to his son-in-law, Ron Spencer, a member of the Yuma Jaycee Foundation, and asked him if the foundation might be interested in this effort since the Jaycees had been one of the original sponsors of the endurance flight. Ron replied that he thought they might be interested, but he needed more details before presenting the idea to the Jaycees. He felt that they would want to know how much money would be involved, specifically, what the airplane would cost plus an estimate of the cost to refurbish it. Jim Gillaspie was asked to come up with these numbers. Planning numbers were given to Ron, and he started laying the groundwork with other members of the foundation.

The original idea was to bring 56H back to Yuma and restore it as closely as possible to look like it did in 1949. After this was completed, the plane would be placed in a Yuma museum. This resulted in a long dialog that lasted several months between Jim, Mr. Neal, and his son, Chris. During the course of the many conversations and negotiations, it was made clear why the Jaycees wanted this particular airplane. Chris stated that he had read the logbook entries on the three endurance flights, but he didn't realize that the record had been broken on the third flight. Chris was told that the Jaycees wanted to refurbish the aircraft and return it as closely as possible to the 1949 configuration. Therefore, they wanted to buy the airplane without the 180

HP engine, mount, cowling, propeller, floats, skis, and hardware. Then they would have to go and find the original engine type, prop, mount, and cowling to put on the airplane. Chris replied that he had another 1948 Aeronca Sedan and that it had the original engine, mount, prop, and cowling, and that they could have them instead. Chris described the engine as "high time," but he thought that it only had one low cylinder. Jim then requested that Chris determine a price for what the Jaycees wanted.

Finally, on April 19, 1997, Chris called with a price of nineteen thousand dollars. The committee met with Ron Spencer and Garth Worthen of the Jaycee Foundation at Dakotas for lunch, and the price and estimated costs were discussed. Ron and Garth thought that the project was something that the Jaycee Foundation would be interested in, and they would take it to the foundation board. At this meeting, Ron indicated that the Jaycees would be interested in returning 56H to an airworthy condition. Jim pointed out that this was a new ball game—returning it to airworthy status—but one that could be solved with time and money. The question of whether the Neals would be interested in donating the airplane, since the Foundation was a non-profit organization, was raised. Jim was tasked to ask them this question. Ron and Garth asked Jim for his long-term commitment to help bring it back and be involved in the restoration.

LET'S MAKE A DEAL

The price was given to the Foundation, and they agreed to fund the purchase price as well as the cost to go get it. Chris was asked if they might be interested in donating the airplane to the non-profit foundation; and he said that they might be, but he would have to look into it. After checking with their accountant, the Neals decided not to take advantage of that suggestion. The price was further negotiated and reduced to eighteen thousand dollars. Everybody agreed to this price; however, there was five feet of snow on the Neal runway, so there was no hurry to go get it. The foundation established a committee, with Ron Spencer as chairman, Garth Worthen as vice-chairman, and Mary Worthen as treasurer. Ron appointed his wife, Judy, as administrator. A thousand-dollar retainer was sent to the Neals in May, 1997, with the understanding that the balance would be due after inspection of the aircraft. Ron, Judy, and other foundation members met with the attorney, Wayne Benesch, and CPA Calvin Brock on June 26 to seek their guidance on the legality of their plans for the airplane. The plan called for bringing it back to Yuma, restoring it, and eventually giving it to another non-profit organization with a home so that the airplane could be put on long-term display.

During the course of the negotiations, Chris offered to let Jim fly 56H to Yuma, and then they would ship all the components back and forth until everything was in place. The airplane, with the 180 HP engine and thirty-six gallons of usable fuel, only had a safe range of slightly over two hours. At a speed of approximately 105 miles per hour, they would have to land every two hundred miles or so to refuel, which was not desirable. Also, some foundation members felt that there was a risk with flying it back. Ron and Jim investigated options on the most economical and timely method to bring 56H back. The first thought was to haul it back using a trailer. This was ruled out because of the time required and the potential for damage when transporting it on an open trailer. They also considered hiring a professional aircraft mover to pick it up and transport it to Yuma. This option was dropped due to costs and the potential for damage. They looked into the option of renting a one-way moving van. After talking to Gary Magrino and Artie Durazo of Multi-Tech and comparing dimensions of the disassembled airplane and the volumetric capability of a twenty-four-foot Ryder truck, they considered that the best option. Artie gave them a few tips on how to economize the effort, and based on his recommendations, this method was selected. It seems that the cost could have been twice as high as that paid; but Ryder had an oversupply of trucks in the East, and they wanted to get them west. Multi-Tech had a need for a truck of this size, so everyone was happy.

Ron and Jim developed a plan that called for hanging the wings on the side of the van and placing the fuselage in between. The tail feathers, cowling, fairings, and other items would be placed on the floor underneath the fuselage. The biggest problem would be securing everything. There have been stories of how aircraft, which were carried this way but not properly secured, were pounded to pieces due to the relative light weight of the airplane and the stiff suspension of the truck. This plan also called for Jim and Ron to travel to Phoenix by shuttle van and then fly by commercial air to Minneapolis. They would take tools with them and rent a truck there. After picking up the airplane, they would drive back to Yuma. One problem remained: where to put the airplane after getting it back to Yuma. Jim, who had been keeping Bill Jewett aware of the progress of this effort, mentioned this to Bill, a big supporter, and he graciously volunteered his warehouse.

By this time, interest was building in Yuma. Reactions ranged from disbelief to pure excitement that indeed there was such an airplane. Ron had contacted KYMA and the *Yuma Daily Sun* and told them what was about to happen. They responded by doing interviews. Pam Smith of the *Sun* interviewed Ron and Jim for a story to be released just before their return to Yuma. She also contacted the newspaper in Staples, Minnesota, and told them what was happening and asked them to photograph the disassembly and loading of the airplane.

FINALIZING THE DEAL

Ron and Jim left Yuma with tools in hand on the eighth of July and traveled to Phoenix on the shuttle bus. From there, they flew to Minneapolis. The taxi ride to the Ryder truck agency was pretty exciting. The driver got lost a couple of times, causing Ron and Jim to wonder whether it was possible to "get there from here." Finally, the lost was found, and they arrived at the Ryder Truck rental station. After renting the truck and padding, they proceeded to drive toward Staples, 120 miles away, via U.S. 10. A few miles outside of Minneapolis, they hit a rough section of highway that caused them to question why they were there. The highway was so rough that the truck, heavily sprung and capable of hauling twenty-six thousand pounds, could not be driven faster than thirty-five miles an hour. Ron said that they needed seat belts just to stay in the truck. Maybe the guys who had problems hauling aircraft that way knew what they were talking about. They persevered and continued on and stopped for the night in St. Cloud. Enough for one day!

Up early the next day, they continued on. The plan was to arrive early that morning in Staples. Once in Staples, they were to call the Neals for instructions on how to get to their house. They lived eight miles west and north of Staples. Jim tried to call several times but got no answer. They figured it was no problem, and they could find somebody who knew them and get instructions to their farm. Several businessmen were asked, but nobody knew them. That seemed unusual. Later, they saw a hardware store and immediately thought that the people there would know the Neals, because all farmers need a hardware store. That may be true, but it turned out that this farmer evidently didn't need that store—they had never heard of the Neals. This left Ron and Jim scratching their heads, but it wasn't a complete loss because they were able to buy eye screws, nails, and other items necessary to secure the airplane, if they ever found it. At this point, they were beginning to question if there was really a farm with 56H sitting on it. Jim remembered that, when negotiating with Chris, he had mentioned Verndale, Minnesota, as being close to their farm, so they decided to drive to Verndale, which was eleven miles west and north of Staples. They stopped at a convenience store on the east end of town and tried to call the Neals once again. Nobody answered the phone. They waited five minutes and called again; there was still no answer. Jim, callused and hardened by this time and expecting a negative answer, asked the clerk if she knew where the Neal farm was located. Surprisingly, she said yes and proceeded to tell them how to get there. But she got confused, and again they wondered if they could "get there from here." Finally, Jim tried the phone once again and this time got Mrs. Neal who gave them clear instructions on how to get to the farm. Within ten minutes, they were driving down the long, built-up dirt road leading to the farmhouse. By this time, and with all the delay and wondering, Ron and Jim were most anxious to see 56H.

As they drove up to the farm, they couldn't see the airplane. This added to their anticipation, but they could see a small closed hangar where they figured it had to be. They knocked on the door, and Mr. and Mrs. Neal greeted them; but Chris wasn't home and wouldn't be back for a while. Chris was to have taken the engine off prior to their arrival, so they expected to catch him working on it. The Neals asked how the trip went. Ron and Jim described trying to reach them, and Mrs. Neal said that she must have been outside when they called. Jim told about how they couldn't find anyone who knew them in Staples. Mr. Neal described how he had lived there all his life, having been born only a mile away. Ron and Jim wanted to see the airplane in the worst way, but they didn't want to seem too anxious. It seemed a long time before Chris returned and opened the hangar. There it was—a beautiful sight, even with the engine cowling off—and it was about to begin its journey back to Yuma. Seeing is truly believing. Jim quickly looked over the exterior then opened the door and climbed in and sat there, quietly savoring the moment for an extended period of time and unaware of what the other people were doing or saying.

THE BONDING

Finally, Jim crawled out of the airplane and then realized what had taken place. He had bonded with 56H, and this was the start of a long relationship. Jim was soon to find out that he wasn't the first to experience such a bond with this airplane. The first task was to verify that this airplane was, indeed, the airplane that had set the record. The first clue was that there were holes in the windshield fairing that offered evidence that two antennas, specially mounted for the endurance flights and shown in the 1949 photos, had been there. Other evidence found was patches over holes in the firewall in which oil lines were routed between the engine and the cockpit. These lines made it possible to add and extract oil from the crankcase. The logbooks were compared to the repairs to fuselage damage and were found to be a reasonable match. The logs indicated that the airplane only had a total of 3,100 hours flying time since it was manufactured in 1948. Bob Woodhouse and Woody Jongeward had flown almost half of those hours. On their first, second, and third attempts, they had flown it 74 hours, then 155, and finally 1,124 hours, for a total of 1,353 hours. In addition, there was the time that they spent experimenting with refueling techniques, deciding how to do that, and then perfecting the technique. The airplane only had 137 hours on it when they started. After making sure that this was the original 56H, Ron and Jim moved it outside, put the cowling back on, and took pictures for a before-and-after sequence.

56H as it looked when it was picked up in Staples, Minnesota, July 8, 1997.

They were in the middle of this when a reporter for the Staples newspaper arrived. Jim wondered how he knew where the Neal farm was. He said that the newspaper had been asked by Pam Smith to cover this event. He started taking pictures, and at the same time, interviewing anybody who would stop and talk to him. The Neals were in awe when the reporter showed up, because of the attention being put on them. They decided that this was such fun that Mrs. Neal called the Wadena newspaper and suggested that they should come out and cover these happenings. They did, so Jim and Ron had to divide their attention between disassembling the airplane and answering questions from two reporters at the same time. They started to take the wings and tail feathers off, and Chris, his dad, and a helper started taking the engine and prop off. After the wings were taken off, they were loaded into the van and secured to the sidewalls with the leading edges down, lightly touching padding that was resting on the floor.

In the middle of the afternoon, Mrs. Neal announced that she had cooked a farm lunch for everybody, including the reporter who was still there. She had prepared ham, quiche, various kinds of vegetables, baked goods, and even a rhubarb pie. The meal was so delicious that the food alone was worth the trip. Mrs. Neal explained, "This is like our dinner. We have a light supper later in the evening." This lunch had a good effect on the reporter because he wrote an amazingly accurate account of what he heard. After eating, Ron and Jim had to develop a way to load the fuselage into the truck. This was solved by driving the truck out into an alfalfa field and backing up to the built-up dirt road leading to the Neals' house. This placed the bed of the truck at about the same level as the road. After removing the engine, they rolled the fuselage out and down the road. At the truck, they turned the fuselage ninety degrees and pushed it into the van while, at the same time, forcing the landing gear together to fit through the door opening.

Loading the fuselage into the Ryder truck, Staples, Minnesota, July 9, 1997.

The tail feathers and other items were loaded under the fuselage. They used eye hooks screwed into the wood floor and tie-downs to secure everything. They worked until approximately 8:00 P.M. Finally, they drove to Staples, where they stayed all night, returning to the farm the next morning to load the engine and the remaining items. The last thing was to complete the paperwork and pay off the balance.

THE LONG ROAD HOME

Ron and Jim left the Neal farm at noon on the tenth of July. They took U.S. 10 northwest to Fargo, North Dakota, and then got on I-94 and drove to Wibaux, Montana. Along the way, the weather turned bad, with thunderstorms, hard rain, and low, dark clouds. Jim said, "One of them looked like a big, rotating tire with bags hanging down out of it. They were all threatening." He was glad that they weren't out there with the airplane on an open trailer. It became a race to get out from under those clouds. They learned later that there was a tornado in the area, but they didn't see it.

The next day they continued west to Billings, Montana, and then joined up with I-90. They stayed on that freeway to Bozeman, then turned south on U.S. 191, passing through Gallatin National Forest, West Yellowstone, and stayed overnight at Idaho Falls, Idaho. When passing through Bozeman, they encountered more washboard roads on which they couldn't go faster than thirty-five miles per hour. Otherwise, the maximum speed that they could go was sixty-five. They had to stop every few miles to inspect everything and make adjustments if necessary. The next day they continued south on   I-15 and spent the night in Las Vegas. The following day they continued south on U.S. 95 and returned to Yuma on Sunday the thirteenth.

An amusing thing happened when they passed through the Arizona inspection station at Ehrenberg, Arizona. The inspector asked, "What you got back there?" Ron answered, "An airplane!" The inspector said, "What?" Ron repeated, "An airplane." The inspector looked kind of puzzled and said, "Oh, well, okay," and waved them through.

THE AIRPLANE RETURNS TO THE PEOPLE OF YUMA

The next day, they unloaded 56H and had an open house so people could see it.

Preparing to unload 56H in Yuma, July 14, 1997. Jim Gillaspie and Bill Cox.

Garth Worthen, Ron Spencer, and Jerry Lillie unloading Fuselage from truck in Yuma.

Ron Spencer and Jim Gillaspie with fuselage after it was off-loaded in Yuma.

The only damage resulting from the move was to the engine baffling. This was easily repaired. Pam Smith's article, "The *City of Yuma* Flying Home," appeared in the *Yuma Daily Sun* on Friday, July 11, 1997. Judy Spencer called a lot of people to come and see it. Young and old alike came to see the airplane. Many old-timers, people who had been in Yuma during the flight, and their sons and daughters—even their grandsons and granddaughters—came and shared their pictures and talked about what they had been doing during that period of time. One of those granddaughters was Marilyn Gardner, whose husband, Greg, of KAWC, worked on the moving crew whenever the airplane was moved around town to various events. Greg has been active with the promotions also, particularly with his radio programs. Marilyn's mother, Betty, is the daughter of Ray Prather, who was involved in transporting the meals to the fliers in 1949.

Shirley Burch with son, Kristoffer, inspecting aircraft after it got back to Yuma.

Participating sons and daughters of those involved in the flight included Judy Spencer, daughter of Horace and Jackie Griffen; Nancy Woodhouse, daughter of Bob; Shirley Burch, whose father, Paul, was the mechanic; Perry Pensky, whose father, Bernie, owned Penn Signs, which made the signs on the airplane and on the refueling car; Garth Worthen, whose father, Charlie, helped build the rack on the refueling car; and Claude Sharpensteen III, whose father was co-owner of the airplane and generously loaned it to the Jaycees. After hearing many stories that were told with affection about all the events that occurred during that period, Jim realized that it really wasn't necessary to reintroduce the airplane to Yuma. The simple truth was that 56H had never left Yuma because it had lived on in the hearts of all these people. One teen-aged boy asked, "Why was the airplane allowed to leave Yuma?" No one could answer his question other than to say, "That's the way they did things in those days." Nobody believes that it will leave Yuma again. Pam Smith came, and on seeing so many sons and daughters of the principal players in 1949 there, she dubbed the group the "Endurance Brats."

THE RESTORATION BEGINS

Work to restore 56H to its glory days was started a short time later. Many volunteers, at times perhaps too many, came forward to help. All ski and float hardware was removed; the instrument panel was replaced; and the fuselage

53

and empennage were prepped for paint. Shirley Burch was especially pleased to be able to use her father-taught skills on this airplane. Among other things, she enjoyed being able to remove a very large rotating beacon that was mounted on the rudder. That beacon was not on 56H in 1949. Shirley also worked on the fuselage, making patches where necessary after the removal of some of the hardware. Sun Western Flyers and Keith Tyree donated materials to repair the fabric. The aircraft was painted in the same color scheme by Jimmy Allen in Tom Pulda's paint booth. (Jimmy, a volunteer, is considered the best painter in Yuma.) Ron Contreras of Penn Signs painted the lettering. Penn Signs did the original painting in 1949 and is the oldest licensed continuously family-owned business in Yuma. The wings were stripped of paint by Bob Schmidgall and then hand-polished by numerous volunteers including the CAP cadets from Yuma Squadron 509.

Jerry McGuire, who owns a part-time business called J&S Sewing, volunteered to rebuild and reupholster the seats and side panels, using FAA-approved materials.

Since the airplane was to be flown again, it was necessary to give it a complete inspection to determine the exact condition. Leak-down tests were given to each cylinder, and three were found to have little capability to hold compression. The engine had a record of being hard on cylinders. Since the engine was close to the recommended overhaul time, a decision was made to tear it down, this being the only way to determine overall condition. The engine was moved to Ernie Muñoz's house where he, John Youkey, and Jim Gillaspie took it apart. They noted the general condition and used micrometers to check critical components to determine the amount of wear. The decision was made to send the crankshaft, camshaft, rods, tapped bodies, crankcase, and other items off to be reconditioned. Jim called Greg Merrill, owner of Aircraft Specialties Services of Tulsa, Oklahoma, to tell him that the items were being shipped to him. At the same time, Jim told him about the famous aircraft that they came from. Greg responded by saying that he was interested in this, and that his company would give the group a reduced price on parts and some free labor. He also said that his company didn't work on crankcases but that DivCo down the street did. Jim called DivCo, talked to Charlie Jarvis, and found out that Greg had already called him. They also gave him a break on the cost of reconditioning the case. In the meantime, Jim Siemens and Jim Gillaspie checked the cylinders and found that four of six were worn beyond limits and needed to be overhauled. The other two had already been bored out because of wear.

Jim called DivCo again—a company that also specializes in cylinder overhaul—and found out that it was cheaper to buy new ones than to overhaul the old ones. Because of this, they contacted Continental Motors about getting new ones. That effort is described in chapter four of this book. All items were sent off, reconditioned, and returned. New bearings, gasket kit, rod bolts and nuts, and other items were purchased. When all components were returned, the engine was moved to Jim Siemens' workshop and reassembled by Ernie Muñoz, Jim Siemens, John Youkey, and at times, Jim Gillaspie. The magnetos were relatively new and didn't require attention. The carburetor venturi and float were changed in accordance with FAA airworthiness directives. The generator and starter were disassembled, inspected, and tested with the help of Jim's Harley Shop and Howard's Alternator and Generator Service. The fuselage was moved to Jim Siemens' house to facilitate hook-up of the engine. The difference in size of the two engines has required replacement of certain items. Ernie Muñoz, FAA-certified mechanic with inspection authorization (IA), headed up this effort.

The engine mount and cowling came from a different airplane, a Canadian one. Since all Aeroncas were individually built by hand, there were slight differences that had to be overcome. The design of the three-point engine mount made it difficult to get all three bolt holes lined up, which is normal. Jim Gillaspie and Bob Martin developed a way to properly line up the mount to the fuselage. The mount was later powder coated, which was arranged by Nick Curtis and accomplished by his sons at Powder Tech in Phoenix. The cowling did not fit properly, so adjustments had to be made by drilling new holes. Two new lower cowl pieces were fabricated by Jim Allen and mated to the rest of the cowling. The cowling then looked even better than when it was new.

The airplane was completely inspected, and corrections were made. A new windshield was installed as well as the side window glass. Carl Franks, a winter visitor from the state of Washington, made a fold-up refueling door similar to the one used in 1949 that was made by Dallas Hovatter. This door will be used when 56H is placed in a museum. Clay Garrison, another winter visitor from Missouri, and Jim Gillaspie resealed the Goodyear brake system. Garth Worthen, in conjunction with Foxworth Lumber, replaced the rear wooden decking. H. G. Frautschy, editor of the Experimental Aircraft Association's magazine, *Vintage Airplane* (circulation: twenty-five thousand), found out about this effort and offered his services. He wrote a brief article about the *City of Yuma* for the January 1999 issue and asked if anyone had certain items that they would like to donate. This included flying wires, an instrument light, and control wheels. Original control wheels were donated by D. Carlson of Hay Springs, Nebraska. Other items were contributed by readers in Rhode Island and Missouri. These items are rare and would have been difficult to find otherwise.

Other contributors and volunteers donating time, energy, and material to the project included: Ray Williams, western representative for the Arizona Pilots Association; Gary Wedding, owner of the Avionics Shop in Eloy, Arizona, who provided vintage instruments and more; Therole Miller, whose pads were used for transporting the wings and various certified parts for the engine; Bill Wilcox, vintage radio parts and instruments for auction; Jesse Mooneyham, trailer and engine removal; Mike Thompson, YPG Heritage Center Curator, vintage items for auction; and Harold Gelman, who has assisted in locating engine parts and a propeller.

Work continued on the airplane to make it airworthy and operational. Parallel work continued on the engine, completing new baffling and wiring. Wing polishing continued. The pressure to complete this effort in time for the fiftieth anniversary was beginning to mount.

Each wing is equipped with a flat strip of aluminum (tabs) on the trailing edge of the wing tip that is designed to be used as a means to trim the airplane so it flies straight and level. This trim adjustment has to be made on the ground by bending the tabs because there is no means of doing so in the air. When the airplane was bought, the tab on the right wing was bent up, and the one on the left wing bent slightly down. Jim Gillaspie assumed that this was necessary to correct for the aerodynamic effects of the floats. The decision was made not to change them at that time.

The fuselage was moved to Jim Siemens' garage to begin the mating process of the engine to the fuselage. The team burned the midnight oil many nights due to the changes required by the differences between the Continental and Lycoming engines. When that was completed, the engine was started, and it ran perfectly. Now the cowling was ready for the final fitting process. This, of course, was not easily accomplished and required more time. Finally, after all adjustments were made, the reconditioned propeller was installed, and the fuselage looked complete again. Upholstery and carpeting were completed and installed.

Martha and Ellis Taylor, owners of Bet-Ko Air, graciously allowed the use of their hangar for final assembly. This effort began on the nineteenth of August. Dick Rautenberg transported the fuselage on one of his vehicle recovery trucks, and the wings and empennage were moved on a separate trailer by the usual supporting crew. This crew varied from one move to another, but it consisted of Greg Gardner, Buddy Dean, Garth Worthen, Bill Cox, Ron Zimmerman, Craig Rundle, Jerry Lilley, Walter Aims, Carl Franks, Shirley Burch, Terry Matzner, Jesse Mooneyham, Matt Matlock, Rudy Schantek, Glen LaHaise, and Clay Garrison. Jesse Mooneyham, Therole Miller, Porky Pierson, and McNeece Brothers Oil Co. provided trailers to assist in these moves.

ASSEMBLING AND FINAL INSPECTION

Thus began the time-consuming effort of assembling the entire airplane, checking and rechecking every connection. Weight and balance checks were made on September sixth and then again on the eighth. On the thirteenth of September, the airplane appeared ready for a high-speed taxi test and braking tests were conducted. Adjustments were made to the noisy brakes, which is characteristic of the older-type Bendix disc brake assemblies.

Jimmy Allen, painter of airplane, and Ron Contreras of Penn Signs, who did all the artwork, just as the company had done in 1949.

Close-up of front of airplane, showing new cylinders and newly-refinished prop.

The *City of Yuma* sitting out on the line at Bet-Ko Air, ready for the fiftieth
anniversary flight, October 10, 1949.

Instrument panel showing brass plaque, very much as it was in 1949.

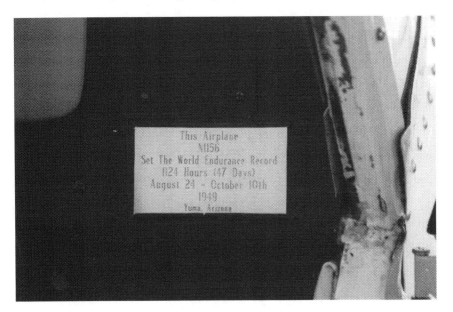

Brass plaque close-up.

Bob and Woody showing their names on airplane, October 8, 1999.

Close-up of Woody and Bob seated in airplane, October 8, 1999.

Bob, Jim Gillaspie (pilot for anniversary reenactment), and Woody, answering questions, October 8, 1999.

On the morning of the fourteenth, a decision was made to conduct a high-speed taxi on runway 17. The wind was approximately three to four knots from thirty degrees, which meant a slight quartering tailwind. Jim Gillaspie made one run at about twenty-five knots, and the airplane moved to the right. It was assumed that a slight gust must have caused that so no more runs were made that day.

The next day, winds were calm and the tower was closed, so Jim took the airplane out to runway 21R and its two hundred-foot width. On the first run, the airplane was accelerated to take-off speed, and the airplane moved to the right. Jim tried to correct with left aileron. The airplane left the ground and, with full left aileron, the airplane slowly drifted to the right. The throttle was closed, and Jim landed the airplane on the right side of the runway. He taxied back to the hangar where Jim Siemens was waiting. They adjusted the trim tabs to where they thought they should be and conducted a second high-speed lateral control check. The adjustments were perfect and the airplane handled properly and was considered airworthy.

THE *CITY OF YUMA* FLIES AGAIN

On September fifteenth, Jim flew the *City of Yuma* on its maiden test flight for forty-two minutes over the airport and made two landings. The airplane was finally ready and all the paperwork was completed.

The *Yuma Daily Sun* wanted air-to-air shots, so Ken Scott volunteered himself and his airplane to get the photos that they wanted. Jim Gillaspie flew the airplane down to the south practice area with Ken Scott and the photographer following and taking photos. They published a photo the next day that was picked up and sent around the world. A Yuma citizen, returning from Taiwan, picked up a Chinese newspaper that was printed in both English and Chinese and there, to his surprise, was a picture of the *City of Yuma*.

First flight after completion of restoration. Jim Gillaspie flying over practice area south of Yuma International Airport, September 16, 1999.

The next flight was to give Ron Spencer a long-awaited ride. It was on this flight that Jim noticed that the left tank fuel usage appeared to be greater than the right. The airplane's fuel-control system consisted of one on-off valve requiring the tanks to feed the engine together. On most high-wing aircraft with only one valve, one tank will lead the other for a period of time, but after flying for a while, the two tanks will equalize.

Arizona Flyways magazine sent their chief photographer, Bob Shane, to Yuma to get photos of the *City of Yuma*. In the meantime, the publisher of the magazine asked Jim Gillaspie to write an article for the October 1999 issue.

Bob and his friend, Ron Kilbry, who was to write an article about the *City of Yuma* for *Plane and Pilot* magazine, went to work. Bob wanted pictures of the airplane in various places and positions. One photo—a shot right at sundown—made the cover of *Arizona Flyways*. He also wanted air-to-air pictures of the *City of Yuma* flying over the sand dunes. He wanted all the shots to be with the airplane flying at approximately five hundred feet above the terrain. Since this was to be farther from the airport than other flights, Jim agreed to do this flight for a limited time only. He also agreed to take Ron Kilbry with him. Since he expected to be gone for only an hour or so, he didn't top off both tanks. Bob enlisted Oray Williams to fly the chase plane. The two airplanes flew out to the sand dunes and started making photo runs as Bob Shane wanted—west-to-west, north-to-south, and all points in between. Jim noticed that the left tank was emptying faster than the right. He told the chase plane that the next run was to be the last, and they agreed. However, at the end of that run, Bob wanted another and then another.

Finally Jim said "No" and added that he was heading back to the airport "right now." The chase plane continued to take pictures back to within five miles of the airport. At that point, they broke off and separated. Jim called Yuma tower and was told to approach from the northwest at 1,200 AGL (above ground level) and turn final, two miles west, for straight in to runway 8. As Jim banked to make the left turn for runway 8, the engine sputtered and died. Jim started the emergency procedure checks, including magnetos and fuel valve settings. At the same time, he looked for a safe place to land. Both fuel gauges showed fuel in their respective tanks, with more in the right than in the left. The engine had started to quit just about even with the blue water tower. Jim picked Avenue A extension south of the Border Patrol facility since the runway was too far away.

All Jim could think about was not putting the airplane in harm's way. He didn't want to live with that the rest of his life. As he rolled the airplane level from the turn, the engine came back to life and started to sputter again as he worked the throttle open and closed. With each sputter, the airplane was getting lower and closer to runway 8, reaching a point where Jim knew he could make the runway even if the engine quit again. At about that point, the engine started running smoothly, making the landing uneventful. Something was obviously wrong with the fuel system. The engine ran perfectly during taxi back to the hangar. The left fuel gauge showed less than five gallons available; however, upon closer examination of the tank, only one gallon remained in the left tank. Apparently, when the aircraft was in the left bank, the right tank hadn't supplied enough fuel to keep the engine running.

The family of Bob Woodhouse wasn't too keen about Bob flying the airplane during the fiftieth anniversary demonstrations, so Jim Gillaspie volunteered. On the third of October, Jim asked Bob if he would like to fly the airplane. Bob responded, "Yes!" He got in the pilot's seat with Jim next to him, and away they went. Jim reported that Bob flew the airplane so well that it was hard to believe that he hadn't been in it for fifty years. Bob remembered where everything was located as though it were tattooed on his brain. They flew for two hours at low level, calling on almost every farmhouse in the Mohawk Valley. Bob made a perfect wheel landing on Larry Boyd's 2,200-foot dirt strip in the Dome Valley and on returning to Yuma. There was no doubt that he could fly that airplane.

The next series of flights was in preparation for the fiftieth anniversary, and they are described in chapter four, "Publicity in an Effort to Pay the Bills."

CHAPTER FOUR

PUBLICITY IN AN EFFORT TO PAY THE BILLS

The return of the *City of Yuma* and its restoration efforts were supported, and in many ways made possible, by the tenacity of the promotional group, consisting mainly of Ron and Judy Spencer.

Ron and Judy worked in many capacities on the committee, which took them in various directions, including making presentations to civic groups, writing letters, making hundreds of phone calls, producing a monthly newsletter, scheduling numerous appearances of the airplane around the city, and trying to get contributions, major sponsors, and a permanent home for the *City of Yuma*. Jim Gillaspie, Horace Griffen, Garth and Mary Worthen, Nancy Woodhouse, Shirley Burch, Jerry Barnett, and Greg Gardner were involved in many of these efforts, mostly in support roles. The two pilots, Bob and Woody, appeared at some activities, including barbecues and radio and television programs.

HOMELESS AIRPLANE LOOKING FOR A HANGAR

The group was searching for a permanent home for the airplane to be on display even before Ron and Jim went to Minnesota and brought it back to Yuma. They went to the airport authority board on April 30, 1997, because they knew that a new terminal was going to be built.

"We told them that the *City of Yuma* was coming back to Yuma and it could be made available to hang inside the terminal if possible," Ron said. "The board members were interested, but they were afraid that it wouldn't fit inside the building because of the restrictions of the site. Later, they wrote that they wouldn't be able to display the airplane in the new terminal.

"We then pursued another avenue," Ron said. "We went to Joyce Wilson, city administrator, and talked to her. She said that she would approach the Crossing Park and the Madison Avenue Development Group regarding a place for the *City of Yuma.*"

A few weeks later in September, Ron, Judy, and Jim met with Rafael Payan, acquisition and development chief of the State of Arizona Parks Department. Rafael, out of Phoenix, was in Yuma for the day. He liked what they showed him as they discussed having the airplane at the Crossing Park. Later, however, the director of the State Parks Department decided that 56H did not fit into the park's historical theme: "Transportation from 1831 for One Hundred Years."

The group also held conversations with the Historical Society, Carol Brooks in particular, about how to go about getting grants. She gave them what information she could, including people to contact.

"I went to a city council meeting on November 5," Ron continued, "saying that, in 1999, we intend to give the airplane to a qualified organization that would have a home for it to be displayed permanently. The council members all voiced their support to find such a place. Joyce Wilson, city administrator of Yuma, a great supporter of this effort, agreed to try to find a home, but she also said that it might be two or three years before anything develops."

During the course of all these activities, Judy came up with the idea that the committee consider flying the airplane more than once. It could be used to fly to other airports such as Casa Grande and Williams Gateway for their big Experimental Aircraft Association Fly-Ins. This would be a way to promote the airplane and the city of Yuma. Bob Bonham, air show coordinator for the Reno Air Races, expressed interest in having it come to the Reno Air Races someday as an added attraction.

"Also, the Historical Society would like to have the *City of Yuma,* if the Jaycee Foundation could come up with some of the funding for a building that could be located behind the Molina Block," Judy explained. "Presently, there are old apartments there that needed [*sic*] to be torn down. They are willing to give the committee a plot of land to fabricate a new building in which to put the airplane. The society had their architect look at it; and, based upon the dimensions of the airplane, he came up with a building that would be approximately 6,400 square feet. It would be designed as a museum that would hold more than just this airplane. If the money can be raised somewhere, whether through grants or fund-raisers or private donations, that is still a viable option."

"Our first event where the *City of Yuma* was displayed was at the Chili Cook-Off downtown on Madison Avenue on October 25, 1997," Ron said. "The airplane, by that time, was pretty well stripped of its paint. We had the engine in it with no top cowling. Garth Worthen made the photo display boards, and Shirley Burch made the inserts for all the pictures. The picture boards told the story of the flight and getting the airplane back. Paper airplanes, cut out and folded by Shirley Burch and her Cibola High School teacher's assistants, were handed out to all children who attended. These continued to be favorites of young children throughout all occasions when the airplane was displayed. Approximately four thousand of these have been handed out."

LEND A HELPING HAND, PLEASE

A package of information consisting of pictures, video, and documents relating the long history of Yuma's endurance airplane was sent to Continental Engines, Inc. in an attempt to get the company to become a major sponsor, if possible, or to rebuild the existing engine. Initially there was no response, so another package was sent, which finally resulted in a rejection notice. A short time later, Jim and Ed Duppstadt were talking about the situation, and Ed said, "You know, Col. Jim Davis, former post commander at Yuma Proving Ground (YPG), retired from the army and went to work for Continental. In fact, he was one of the vice presidents of the military vehicles part of Teledyne Continental."

Jim Gillaspie placed a call to Jim Davis, who remembered seeing pictures of the endurance flight when he was at YPG. Jim told him that the airplane was back in Yuma and of the committee's attempt to get Continental to help on the engine. Jim Davis replied that he thought he could help. Although he no longer worked for Continental, he was a friend of Carl Bayer, who is CEO of Allegheny Teledyne, Inc., the parent company of Continental. He said that he planned to have lunch with Carl Bayer the following week and would talk to him about the situation. First, however, he wanted the committee to develop ideas on how it would benefit Continental promotionally to be involved in this effort. He said to send him all the ideas and he would get Bayer interested. This was accomplished the following day.

Jim Davis discussed the endeavors of the Yuma group with Carl Bayer, who was interested. He thought that the people at Continental might want to participate in the project and said that he would discuss it with them.

Continental's president sent the question to all his department heads for their opinions. The result of that was a veto by the organization's legal department because of possible liability. The next question from the restoration committee was, "How about parts?" The answer was, "Come to us if you need something."

Later, when the inspection of the cylinders had been completed by Jim and verified by Jim Siemens, it was decided that they needed to be overhauled. Jim Gillaspie called DivCo of Tulsa and found out that nobody overhauled that type of cylinder anymore because it was considerably cheaper to buy new ones. Ed Duppstadt approached Continental again by way of Jim Davis who, in turn, talked to Carl Bayer. Nothing was heard for a while; so Ed, who was "leading the charge," called to see what the response was. He talked to the president's secretary, who said that she would see about getting some help for the group.

A short time later, Continental sent a letter that said that the group could buy the cylinders at a reduced price ($597 instead of $750, plus shipping), and the company would waive the core charge of $150 per cylinder. Continental did not place any special requirements, such as promotion, on the committee.

In November the airplane was on display at the Colorado River Balloon Festival at Cibola High School. Ron continued to tell the *City of Yuma*'s story and explain the need for a permanent display, which he described as follows:

"In December we contacted State Senator Jim Carruthers and set up a luncheon on the twentieth at the Crossing Restaurant. We told him what we were doing, what we intended to do, and that we needed a home for the airplane. As a result, a little later, Jim Carruthers mentioned the armory downtown and said that it might be vacated by the National Guard and he thought that the structure was going back to the city of Yuma. He said, 'You know, that would be the perfect place to build a museum.' So that's another possibility."

The first public event of 1998 at which the *City of Yuma* was on display was the Old Time Fiddlers' Contest in downtown Yuma in January. The group had a booth with storyboards and advertising merchandise for sale— tee shirts, caps, and mugs.

McNeece Brothers Oil Company generously provided a trailer to transport the airplane to numerous events around town throughout the restoration and promotion process.

SPECIAL APPEARANCES

On February 7, 1998, 56H was in the Silver Spur Rodeo Parade. A work crew moved the airplane from Bill and Barbara Jewett's warehouse to the parking lot at Beeler Equipment Company on Porky Pierson's trailer. There they mounted the wings and tail feathers back onto the fuselage in the dark. The appearance of the airplane in the parade was not widely known in advance. People couldn't believe what they were seeing as it went along the parade route. After the parade ended, the group took the wings off at the south end of Main Street and moved the fuselage, storyboards, and merchandise to Main and Second Streets, where the old Valley Café used to be. Some of these events were not very productive in regard to selling merchandise, but at least word about the airplane was being circulated.

The following weekend, February 13–15, the airplane and merchandise were at the Silver Spur Rodeo. "Yuma Crossing Days happened to be the same weekend," Ron said, "and Mary Worthen went to that and took some of the merchandise."

On March 6–8, the famous Aeronca was on display at the annual car show, "Midnight at the Oasis," sponsored by the Caballeros de Yuma where they had over seven hundred cars on display. The *City of Yuma* had its wings on and cowlings in place.

The group had thoughts of applying in 1998 for a historical preservation grant with the state of Arizona. The first step would have been to get the *City of Yuma* into the registry of historic places and things, for which it would have been eligible in 1998, as it was built in 1948 and the minimum required age was fifty years. When they started, they were told that they had to wait until the historical *event* was fifty years old; since the flight was in 1949, no further action was taken.

RAISING MONEY THROUGH VARIOUS ACTIVITIES

The group developed plans for a benefit dinner and auction to be held at Bill and Lois Britain's Tumbleweed Chuckwagon in April, as well as a golf tournament. Nancy Woodhouse led the charge for the dinner and auction, and Perry Pensky did that for the golf tournament. Prior to the dinner, Ron and Judy received a phone call from Jacques Istel, who built the Center of the World tourist attraction at the edge of the sand dunes west of Yuma. He had heard about the benefit dinner and auction, and he wanted to donate the two pilots' names and two others to be engraved on the wall located there at Felicity. This opportunity would be auctioned off. The offer was accepted, and Bob and Woody's names are now engraved on the wall.

"We had interviews on several radio programs during the countdown to the benefit barbecue and the golf tournament on April 17 and 18, respectively," Ron said. John Phipps interviewed Horace Griffen, Jim Gillaspie, and Ron Spencer on his *Talk of Yuma* radio program on KJOK on April 14, and then he interviewed Horace Griffen, Woody Jongeward, Nancy Woodhouse, and Dallas Hovatter on April 16. Then in early May, Ron and Jim Gillaspie did a forty-five-minute taped interview with Kim Sanchez of KTTI radio. This was aired on KBLU as well as on KTTI.

Night shot at Britains' Tumbleweed Chuckwagon, March 13, 1999. Left to right, Horace and Jackie Griffen, George and Shirley Murdock, Bob Woodhouse, Jim and Karen Gillaspie.

Griff, Woody, Bob, and Dr. Irwin at Britains' Tumbleweed Chuckwagon, April 17, 1998. Photo by Pam Smith.

The dinner and auction at the Britains' drew approximately 340 people, and considerable money was raised for the restoration of the airplane. This was a success largely due to Bill and Lois Britain, Bobby Brooks, Mayor Marilyn Young, the city council, and John Phipps.

The moving crew took the airplane to the Britains' on April 16, moved it back to the Jewetts' warehouse on April 18, moved it to Tom Pulda's Paint and Body shop on May 1 to be painted, and back again to the warehouse on May 4. On with the wings and back off with the wings every time it made an appearance! The crew, by this time, had become very proficient at moving the airplane and installing and removing the wings and tail feathers. This crew has varied from one move to the next but has consisted of: Greg Gardner, Buddy Dean, Garth Worthen, Bill Cox, Ron Zimmerman, Craig Rundle, Jerry Lilley, Walter Aims, Carl Franks, Shirley Burch, Terry Matzner, Jesse Mooneyham, Matt Matlock, Rudy Schantek, Gene LaHaise, and Clay Garrision. Jesse Mooneyham, Therole Miller, Porky Pierson, and McNeece Brothers Oil Co. have provided trailers to assist in these moves.

Perry Pensky was chairman of the 1949 Endurance Classic Golf Tournament at Desert Hills Municipal Golf Course on April 18. Helping him were Ron Contreras and Kay Nance of Penn Neon Sign Co., Inc. Twelve teams of four took part in the competition, and there were fifteen tee sponsors. That was a successful venture, which provided a good day's activities and raised additional funds.

Ron gave talks to Kiwanis and Rotary Club chapters, and Horace Griffen joined him for a meeting of the Colo-Gila Kiwanis Club. Ron also talked to the historical society and the Experimental Aircraft Association (EAA) Yuma Chapter 590. He talked about how the committee needed the EAA's expertise and support for the project. The chapter, consisting of thirty members, designated Ken Scott as its representative to the committee.

Dan Marries, Bob Woodhouse, and Ron Spencer were guest speakers for Louise Knepper's fourth grade class at Carver School. Dan showed the KYMA documentary, and Bob spent about thirty minutes talking to the kids and answering their questions. The next day, the same class went on a field trip to see the *City of Yuma*. Jim and Bob were both there along with Ron. "They answered a lot of interesting and entertaining questions," Ron said.

On May 13 the historical society had a "Rock Around the Block" fund-raising party in the old McDonald's department store building in downtown Yuma. "We took the fuselage and our souvenir merchandise there," Ron explained. "About 150 to 200 people attended that event. It was a nice party, and we had a good time. They had a 1950s theme with old cars, and the airplane fit right in."

In June 1998, ABC television affiliate channel 15 (Yuma cable channel 5) in Phoenix aired a segment that was taped in April consisting of an interview with Horace and Jim. The segment was taped for their *Arizona Short Stories* program. They were in town to tape a feature on the Crossing Park. Ray Smucker heard about their coming and suggested they cover the *City of Yuma* story. Diane Rodriquez, the producer, directed the interviews.

The moving crew putting on the left wing for a public appearance of the *City of Yuma*.

A beautiful 56H, with its new paint job, logos, and the partially polished wings in place, went to a block party downtown on July 3.

"On September 12, 1998, we wrote to Col. Turner at the Marine Corps Air Station asking for their support and help for the observance of our fiftieth anniversary on October 10, 1999. We were asking to use the airfield and hoped that the military would have various static displays of airplanes and equipment," Ron said.

On October 10, 1998, the forty-ninth anniversary was observed at Bet-Ko Air with 150 to 200 people attending. At the anniversary observance, the Yuma High Choralairs performed in their usual enthusiastic and excellent way. The Crossing Restaurant catered the food, and Dan Marries of KYMA was the master of ceremonies. He showed his excellent documentary video about the endurance flight. Ray Smucker and his wife, Nadine, were there from their home in Phoenix. They brought back memories for some and told others how the flight came about. David Schuman was offered a nylon commemorative flight jacket and ticket number one for a flight in the *City of Yuma* as he attained Crew Member status with a generous donation to the restoration fund. In the spirit of a true Yuman, like his family in 1949, he committed himself to earn the leather jacket.

The committee formally thanked Martha Taylor and her crew at Bet-Ko Air for providing the hangar and setting the event up. Sponsors of the event were Coca-Cola, Crystal Waters, Johnny's TV (which provided a big-screen television set on which the documentary video was shown), Fisher Chevrolet, Plaza Auto Center, Sun Valley Beverage, Yuma Crossing Restaurant, Todd Pinnt and the Civil Air Patrol cadets, Jaycee foundation members, the Jaycees, and the Junior Jaycees.

At the end of October, 56H and the commemorative merchandise went downtown for the Historical Society's Chili Cook-Off. Many people commented about the dramatic change that was in evidence after a year of restoration work.

On November 21 and 22, the *City of Yuma* was at the annual Colorado River Balloon Festival at Cibola High School. Helping with the appearance were Claude and Jo Beth Sharpensteen, the Civil Air Patrol Cadets, Nancy Woodhouse, Theresa Buscko, Laura Pully, Judy Spencer, and Elton Worthen.

Ron said, "On January 12, we began to plan an event to observe the fiftieth anniversary of the landing of the *City of Yuma*. We decided to try to have a function at Paradise Casino on the night of October 8, with entertainment representing the forties or fifties era. Larry Boyd volunteered to have us come to his farm in the Dome Valley for a breakfast on Saturday morning, October 9. Then we wanted to have a lunch at Somerton. We talked to Stan Lawless about that, and he said, 'Okay.' That evening the Jaycees would host a barbecue dinner, cooked by Chef Elton Worthen, at Bet-Ko Air."

Ron Spencer, Gene LaHaise, Clay Garrison, and Jim Gillaspie with the *City of Yuma* on display at the Jaycees' 1999 Silver Spur Rodeo.

Ron, Jim, and Horace gave a presentation at Cocopah Bend RV and Golf Resort on January 18. Then the airplane was moved to KYMA at the end of January to help them observe their eleventh anniversary.

On February 2, 1999, Jim and Ron took their "wish list" of activities for Sunday afternoon, October 10, 1999, for the observance of the fiftieth anniversary to Lt. Col. Coburn, the operations officer at MCAS. These included a static display with modern and vintage military aircraft if possible, civilian vintage airplanes, possibly some agricultural airplanes, and an AV-8 flying demonstration. Then the *City of Yuma* would fly by at a low altitude, in formation with the 1948 Buick refueling car to simulate a refueling run. Col. Coburn had to obtain official approval from MAWTS, the Military Air Weapons Tactics Squadron; because at that time their weapons tactics training would be going on and they had to be sure that there would be no Sunday afternoon air activity.

Ron said that Lt. Col. Coburn felt that they could work around that. "We asked them if they could take care of tents, seating, and security," Ron continued. "Our merchandise would be there for sale, and we would have a dedication of the airplane to the city of Yuma—probably to Mayor Marilyn Young."

On February 6, 56H was again in the Silver Spur Rodeo Parade with the Civil Air Patrol cadets providing an honor guard. Sellers Petroleum provided a truck and lowboy for that occasion. Then on the twelfth through the fourteenth, the airplane and the souvenir merchandise were on display at the rodeo. On February 20 the airplane was again displayed at the big annual air show at MCAS for Military Appreciation Days.

Transporting both wings for a public appearance. Clay Garrison, Carol Franks, Jim Gillaspie, and Ron Spencer facing camera, Gene LaHaise on near side.

McNeece Brothers Oil Company had offered a stake bed truck to transport the airplane to the air show, but its engine had burned up. Garth Worthen arranged for a truck to take the airplane out to the airport, and Jesse Mooneyham came to the rescue with a trailer to take it back to the Jewetts' warehouse afterward.

Loading the *City of Yuma* to be transported back to the Jewetts' warehouse, Sunday morning, March 14, 1999, after benefit dinner and auction at Britains' Tumbleweed Chuckwagon

REFUELING CAR JOINS THE SHOW

The air show was the first event that featured a newly acquired 1948 Buick Super convertible along with the airplane. George Murdock had been looking for a car like the first new one that he had bought as a young man. He remembers that he paid $2,800 for that new Buick convertible. Milton Phillips, regional authority on old cars, had helped him search for one over the years and finally located this one in Carmel, California. Milton would have liked to buy the car himself, but he knew how much George wanted one. He drove out to George and Shirley's home in Roll and told them about it. Within minutes, Milton made the deal in a phone call to Carmel. George bought the car, sight unseen, on the basis of the description by his friend, Milton, who then arranged to have the car shipped to Yuma. The fifty-one-year-old Buick was in excellent condition with its original dark green paint; but as George said, "It needs to be white," as his original car (the refueling car) had been. George Murdock restored it. He loaned the car to the committee for the events following its arrival in Yuma and for the observance of the fiftieth anniversary. Tom Pulda's Body Shop and Jimmy Allen prepared the car for painting, and Jimmy painted it. Dave Garcia, owner of Dave's Auto Glass, restored the interior of the car with red leather seats and red carpeting.

The Buick convertible attracted a lot of attention along with 56H at the air show, and the same thing happened at the car show, "Midnight at the Oasis." The beautifully restored airplane and the dark green convertible were displayed together on the expansive lawn at Caballero Park. They attracted a host of admirers. The various commemorative items were sold, and donations were gratefully accepted.

In publicizing the dinner and auction on March 13, Bob Woodhouse and Ron were interviewed by John Phipps on his *Talk of Yuma* program on KJOK, by R. J. Bones at KTTI radio, and by Dan Marries at KYMA.

"At our dinner and auction," Ron said, "we had a good time, and we made a profit at both events. The Fort Yuma Rotary Club solicited items for the auction and took care of the ticket sales. John Phipps and Christy Jo Johns did the auction for us." John and Christy Jo both had the auctioneer's language mastered, which was entertaining and effective. Bobby Brooks cooked delicious tri-tips, and Mayor Marilyn Young and other members of the city council served the food. The Civil Air Patrol cadets were there in their uniforms. It was a special occasion.

The *City of Yuma* on McNeece Brothers Oil Co. truck for transport across town,
March 14, 1999.

Loading the airplane onto the lowboy for the start of a 47-hour "Endurance Sit-In"
by KTTI disc jockeys Eric Bowan and R. J. Bones.

Keeping track of the finances along the way—income and expenditures, bank account business, financial statements, and treasurer's reports at the monthly meetings—was no small matter. Mary Worthen was treasurer of the committee.

"On March 26, we received a check from TOSCO Corporation and Union Oil in the amount of twenty-five hundred dollars," Ron said. "We had a picture taken for the *Yuma Daily Sun* with Mackie Gill of Sellers Petroleum presenting the check."

On April 14 Erik Bowan and R. J. Bones of KTTI had decided to put on another endurance event. They would stay in the airplane for forty-seven hours and attract attention through their broadcasting to try to raise another five thousand dollars. At 4:00 P.M. on May 6, the Forty-Seven-Hour Endurance Day started. Their plan was to stay in the airplane until 3:00 P.M. on May 8. When they were just fifteen minutes shy of their "escape time," they were still short of their target amount of five thousand dollars. Bill Ruch from the House of Vacuums and David Schuman from Farmers Insurance drove into the parking lot and wrote the checks that were needed to bring the total to their five-thousand-dollar goal.

The *City of Yuma* during forty-seven-hour Endurance Sit-In by Eric Bowan and R. J. Jones of KTTI. May 6–8, 1999.

"On May 18," Ron said, "we met with Paradise Casino people, and they gave us some good suggestions. Soon after that they obtained the approval from the tribal council so that they could conduct a big event on the evening of October 8."

During the years of the existence of the Yuma Municipal Airport building, a hand-painted mural on the wall showed the incorrect information that the *City of Yuma* flew 1,008 hours, rather than the correct figure of 1,124 hours. That error carried over into the new terminal and had to be corrected later. This was done, and the 1949 world endurance flight record is now shown correctly.

At a June 24, 1999, meeting, it was decided that the fiftieth anniversary activities would be held at Bet-Ko Air in lieu of the marine base or the new terminal. Present at that meeting were Lucy Shipp of the Yuma County Board of Supervisors; Lt. Col. Coburn and Capt. Jimenez of MCAS Yuma; Ed Thurman, David Gaines, and Daren Griffin, of the Yuma County Airport Authority; Chauncy Dunstan and Mike Covery of Caballeros de Yuma; Martha Taylor of Bet-Ko-Air; Ken Scott of Chapter 590, Experimental Aircraft Association; and Dustin Dinwiddie, of the Civil Air Patrol Cadet Squadron 509, Yuma.

The Caballeros de Yuma made a commitment to help with the fiftieth anniversary celebration on October 8, 9, and 10. Chauncey Dunstan was named as their delegate to work with Ron and Judy Spencer and their group.

Several people donated a few thousand hours each, and many gave hundreds of hours in the restoration and promotion of the *City of Yuma*. The original flight required the time and effort of a large number of volunteers for less than a year, and everything subsequent to that took a smaller number of people a much longer period of time.

FIFTIETH ANNIVERSARY PLANS

In preparation for the fiftieth anniversary, Shirley Murdock wrote invitations to several aviation-oriented magazines to come and cover the event. She had an affirmative response from Russ Munson of *Flying* magazine. Russ, a contributing editor at that time, planned to fly his Piper PA-18 airplane from New York City to Yuma to cover the events.

Since the anniversary demonstration flights were to be held on the civilian side of the field, primarily at Bet-Ko Air, the airport director wanted the group to get an FAA waiver to put it on. This involved filling out paperwork detailing what, where, and who were involved. In addition Jim Gillaspie developed a safety plan, which spelled out responsible personnel and their actions. Two responsible representatives from two groups were named: Ron Spencer from the Yuma Jaycee Foundation and Charles Marcum, president of Yuma's EAA Chapter 590. Other responsible personnel included Mark Smith, safety officer; Major Bowman, MCAS air boss; Ellis Taylor, owner of Bet-Ko Air; Jim Gillaspie, pilot; and Daren Griffin, deputy airport director. This certificate of waiver was granted by the FAA on September 10, 1999, and was to be effective from 1200 MST to 1700 MST on October 10, 1999.

The fiftieth anniversary was fast approaching. Since Jim was to fly formation with the Buick, driven by Horace Griffen, during the simulated refueling runs, it was decided that practice was needed. The runways at Yuma International were too busy to allow something like that, so Judy Spencer contacted Chuck Wullenjohn, public affairs officer of the U.S. Army's Yuma Proving Ground (YPG), about the possibility of practicing at Laguna Army Airfield. Chuck got Col. Robert Filbey's permission, and the date was set for October 5.

George and Shirley Murdock drove the recently restored Buick to YPG where they met Horace Griffen and Ron and Judy Spencer. Jim Gillaspie and Jim Siemens flew out in the *City of Yuma*. After they arrived, a briefing was held to determine how the practice would be done. It was decided that runway 24 would be used. The winds were variable at about six knots out of 330 degrees (a slight crosswind). Horace was to position the Buick at the approach end of runway 24, off to the right side, so that he could see the airplane approach from over his left shoulder. It was up to him to determine the time to start acceleration to get up to sixty-five mph. The airplane was to make a left-hand traffic pattern. Ideally, by this time the airplane would be abreast of the car. Timing was everything because the airplane's stall speed was fifty-nine mph. If the airplane got ahead of the car, it couldn't slow down and wait. Besides, the runway was six thousand feet long, and one could soon run out of runway. Ron Spencer drove the photo chase vehicle with Ed Duppstadt and Judy taking pictures.

The first couple of runs resulted in the airplane outrunning the car; so it was decided that the pilot would tell Horace when to start his run, and the two would join up about halfway down the runway. This worked a little better, but the crosswinds picked up, which presented a problem. The Buick was on the upwind side and, at times would blank out the wind, the airplane would lose partial lift, and the wheels would touch the ground. The crosswind made it difficult to land the tail-dragger. On the last landing, a gust picked up the right wing, requiring full aileron deflection. To counteract it, Jim had to face the airplane directly into the wind. The airplane finally came to a stop at the right edge of the runway. After that they decided to call it a day, primarily because the Buick was starting to overheat. The airplane's left fuel tank was almost empty; very little fuel was used from the right tank because of the engine's tendency to only burn fuel from the left tank. Jim wanted enough fuel added to it to get back to Yuma International Airport. Ron made arrangements to buy ten gallons from the army. They decided to down the airplane when it arrived back at the airport in order to resolve this problem.

The next day, October 6, Jim Gillaspie, Ron Spencer, Jim Siemens, and John Youkey, met at the airplane to figure out what the problem was. The *City of Yuma* had been modified with metal tanks that had an FAA standard-type certificate. This was considered a major improvement over the old bladder-type tanks. The vents for these tanks stick straight forward from the wing in order to get induced air to pressurize the tanks to insure good fuel flow. A pressure check was made on both tanks, and the right one was found to be defective. The gasket was changed, and the problem was resolved. The engine had quit because in the turn the left wing and the tank, which was properly pressurized, were down and gas no longer covered the outlet fitting. The right tank could not meet the demand due to lack of adequate pressure to keep the engine running when the wings were not level.

Russ Munson flew in that day from New York and proceeded to take numerous pictures of the *City of Yuma* and of Bob Woodhouse, Woody Jongeward, and Horace Griffen. Russ asked to take air-to-air photos of the *City of Yuma* with Bob and Woody flying. Bob and Woody agreed, so it was scheduled for Sunday morning, October 10. The plan called for Jim Gillaspie to fly Russ's Super Cub with Russ taking the photos and the two airplanes flying in formation.

After the fuel problem was solved, the team scheduled more practice runs at YPG; but high winds prevailed through Friday, October 8, putting a damper on any more runs. Time was running out. At least the airplane was airworthy and ready for the weekend events.

Therole Miller, John Youkey, and Ernie Muñoz working on engine timing, October 10, 1999.

Planning for the fiftieth anniversary called for activities on the eighth, ninth, and tenth. This planning called for Winterhaven, Somerton, and Wellton, as well as Yuma, to join in the celebration. On Friday night, the eighth, Paradise Casino hosted a big fund-raising affair with a swing show, featuring music from the forties and fifties. Cesar Casillas was the master of ceremonies. Irene Moreno, Jimmy Allen, Mike Thompson, and Ron and Judy Spencer helped the casino prepare for the show. Special guests included Woody Jongeward and Horace Griffen. The theme of the show was "Swing with the *City of Yuma.*" Dress and costume contests were held, and vintage cars were on display. The *City of Yuma,* with Jim Gillaspie and Carl Franks, flew over the proceedings at 6:15 P.M. Councilman Bobby Brooks presented a fiftieth anniversary cake to the group.

Bob, Griff, and Woody at breakfast fly-in, Larry Boyd's farm October 9, 1999.

George Murdock, Judy and Ron Spencer, Woody, and Bob at Boyd's farm.

A variety of airplanes at Boyd's farm.

Jim Gillaspie and John Youkey coming in for landing at Somerton Airport for fly-in lunch served by the Campesinos Sin Fronteras, with Augustin Tumbaga as their head man, October 9, 1999.

On Saturday morning, a fly-in—and drive-in—pancake breakfast hosted by the Wellton-Mohawk Valley Kiwanis Club was held at Larry Boyd's farm in the Dome Valley. There were vintage cars and airplanes on display. The vintage airplanes flew out in a group from Yuma and from Imperial, California. The airplanes and owners attending were Larry Boyd and his 1946 Beech Staggerwing, Bruce Massey and his 1948 Cessna 170, Jeff Jaquay and his 1946 Aeronca Wagon, Larry Roe and his DeHavilland Beaver (L20), and Jim Ehrhart and his 1946 Cessna 140. There were also a couple of other airplanes there that were flown in by neighbors from the Wellton area. Vintage cars included George Murdock's 1947 Buick. Ken Scott and the Yuma Civil Air Patrol Squadron 508 Cadets were responsible for parking the arriving airplanes.

Unfortunately, Bob and Susan Eaton made their last landing in their beautiful Stinson that morning. On touchdown the aircraft drifted to the left and hit a berm, folding up the landing gear. The airplane was a total loss. They were not hurt, but Susan's right foot was pinned in the wreckage. She ran around with her right foot shoeless until Marilyn Boyd loaned her a shoe and she ate breakfast.

The plan called for the *City of Yuma* to arrive after all the other airplanes had landed. As Jim Gillaspie and Jim Siemens cleared the Gila Mountains, they could hear Ken Scott tell the other airplanes to be cautious of the crashed airplane near the end of the runway. That bit of news upset Jim Gillaspie and caused him to make a bad approach and subsequent bad touchdown, making a go-around necessary. The second landing was much better. A good breakfast was served and everybody had a good time in the heat.

That afternoon at Stan Lawless's Somerton AirPlay Airport, lunch was available, sponsored by the Campesinos Sin Fronteras and Augustin Tumbaga, president. Mr. Tumbaga was also mayor of Somerton. In fact, many of the vintage airplanes were based there. Entertainment was provided by the skydivers of Arizona AirPlay. The temperature at that time was hovering around one hundred degrees, which put a damper on the events. Nevertheless, the food was delicious, and everybody had a good time.

That night an outstanding barbeque dinner, sponsored by Jaycee Foundation, was held at Bet-Ko Air. Elton Worthen cooked for the event, with help from his brothers, Garth and Joe, and their families. Approximately six hundred people were served. Ron Spencer was the master of ceremonies. All the visiting dignitaries were introduced. Special guests included Charlie Neal and his wife, former owners of the *City of Yuma*. This was the first time that they had seen the airplane since Ron and Jim took it from their farm near Verndale, Minnesota, and it was quite a change for them.

Charlie Neal of Minnesota, former owner of airplane, October 9, 1999.

TEN-TEN, NINETY-NINE

Early the next morning, a very warm October 10, Bob, Woody, Jim, and Russ Munson met to fly the air-to-air photo mission. Bob flew the *City of Yuma*, and Jim flew the yellow Super Cub. Both airplanes took off to the north on runway 35. The Super Cub took off first with the *City of Yuma* trailing behind. They climbed to one thousand feet above the Bard Valley. The Super Cub was lead, and Bob and Woody flew in formation off the right side. The Cub's right door was opened, allowing Russ unrestricted view of Bob and Woody. Without hesitation, Bob tucked the left wing of the *City of Yuma* right between the Cub's wing and the horizontal stabilizer, as he had learned to do when flying for the navy fifty-five years earlier. Bob's skill allowed Russ to get many outstanding air-to-air photos of Bob and Woody showing their pearly whites. Several of these photos were included in the article that Russ wrote for *Flying* magazine that hit the newsstands in February 2000. Later that morning, Bob and Woody and their wives were interviewed for documentary purposes at Nancy Woodhouse's home, where she served a big breakfast.

In the meantime, preparations were underway at Bet-Ko Air for the refueling run demonstrations. The Marines were moving their display aircraft to the civilian side of the field. Included were one AV8B Harrier, one F5 Freedom Fighter, and the air station's search-and-rescue helicopter. The Caballeros de Yuma, with Chauncey Dunstan and Don Eskam leading, were getting ready to handle parking and other concessions. The Jaycee Foundation crews were erecting the speakers' stand and seating and preparing the concession stands. The Marine Corps Band members were offloading their instruments and selecting locations to set up; and the Civil Air Patrol cadets, with Todd Pinnt leading, were determining how to handle the influx of aircraft expected to arrive. Access to taxiway India 2 from Bet-Ko Air was blocked, which required all aircraft coming and going from Bet-Ko Air to use India 3 taxiway. The master of ceremonies, Frank Kingston Smith, who volunteered his time, was being briefed by Ron and Judy Spencer. Judy was also collecting all the guest speakers who were scheduled to say a few words.

Planning called for the demonstration to start at noon. There were to be three segments, each with three runs. The first segment was to take place at noon, the second at 1:30 P.M., and the third at 3:00 P.M. The demonstration runs were to be conducted on runway 35 (northbound.) The airplane was to approach from the south. The refueling Buick, with Horace Griffen driving and crewed by George Murdock, Chuck Mabery, and John Youkey (radioman), was to position on the runway overrun and wait for the call from Jim Gillaspie. Dick Rautenberg provided the photo chase truck and was to stay on the Buick's right side throughout the run sequence. At the end of the run, the *City of Yuma* would pull up and fly around the pattern to position for another run. The Buick and chase truck would return to the south end of the runway and get ready for a repeat.

Simulated refueling run on fiftieth anniversary: Jim Gillaspie as pilot, Bob Woodhouse with him, Horace Griffen driving refueling car, John Youkey as radioman, Chuck Mabery standing with fuel can, and George Murdock in backseat, October 10, 1999.

George Murdock with fuel can and refueling car.

Shot of simulated refueling, taken from Dick Rautenberg's truck with Dick driving, Jim flying, Bob riding along as passenger, Griff driving refueling car, George standing, and John serving as radioman.

United States Marine Band at fiftieth anniversary celebration, October 10, 1999.

Overview at anniversary celebration.

Bob and Woody shaking hands on "Ten-Ten Ninety-Nine."

The fiftieth anniversary celebration got underway with the Marine band playing a selection of music including "The Star Spangled Banner." Marine Corps Air Station Yuma commanding officer Col. Mark Condra attended the celebration and was part of the ceremony that dedicated the restored *City of Yuma* to the people of Yuma County.

Temperature at the time of the first run was approximately 105 degrees. The Buick and the chase truck were first to leave the parking area, followed by the *City of Yuma,* under the direction of the Civil Air Patrol Cadets. The airplane, with Jim Gillaspie and Jim Siemens aboard, took off on runway 35 heading north. At the proper altitude, the airplane turned crosswind and left downwind for 35. Jim kept the tower informed as they proceeded around the pattern. When they were ready to turn "final," the tower approved the run. The lack of practice showed, with the airplane overrunning the Buick because of shifting problems, and at times acceleration was hesitant. This car was fifty years old and probably had not been driven that hard, ever. Regardless, the runs clearly showed the difficulty in such a maneuver, making a car and an airplane match speed in less than five thousand feet. Jim Gillaspie asked Bob Woodhouse to accompany him on the next three runs. Bob was overjoyed at being asked to go. There must have been some kind of magic with Bob being in the airplane, because those were the best runs of the day. When the Buick returned from those runs, somebody noticed that the left front tire was going flat. A team of volunteers jumped in and helped George change the tire, a moment reminiscent of 1949 when George had to keep the car running at all costs.

For the third sequence, Jim Siemens returned to the cockpit, carrying a video camera to capture a bird's-eye view of the airplane approaching the car. Because of time constraints, only two runs were made on the third and final segment. Unknown to the crowd, Bob and Woody got in the airplane and took off, with the intention of landing at the precise time that they landed fifty years before. This they did, to the delight of the crowd, which by this time had thinned due to the heat.

Standing: Chris Bean, Jim Siemens, Judy Spencer, Jim Gillaspie, Martha and Ellis Taylor. In front: John Youkey and Ron Spencer.

Martha and Ellis Taylor, owners of Bet-Ko Air, where the airplane was housed from September 1999 through 2005.

After the runs, the many photographers present took numerous pictures of various people at the event. This probably lasted for an hour or more. By this time, everybody was tired and couldn't wait to get home, but first things had to be returned to their proper locations on both sides of the air station.

Principal players at the fiftieth anniversary celebration. John Youkey, Jimmy Allen (of the Yuma Jaycees) in front, Jimmy Allen (painter of the airplane), Bill Cox, Garth Worthen, Mark Smith (behind Jim Gillaspie), Carl Franks, Woody Jongeward, Horace Griffen, Jim Siemens (behind George Murdock), Bob Woodhouse, and Judy Spencer.

The governor of Arizona, Jane Hull, issued a proclamation that October 1999 was *City of Yuma* Endurance Plane Month.

During the following years, the *City of Yuma* was flown to air shows and other functions nearby in Wellton, Casa Grande, Kingman, Parker, and the Naval Air Station in El Centro, California. The Kingman Air and Auto Show sent a special invitation to the *City of Yuma* to attend its show in 2000. This turned out to be a bittersweet occasion because Charlie Bland, formerly of Yuma, who was living in Kingman and was seriously ill, wanted to see the airplane one last time. Jim and Ron flew to Kingman, not knowing of his desire. On the morning of the air show, Charlie's friends brought him to the airport in a golf cart. Charlie had just enough strength to look at the airplane, and then he had to be taken home, where he later died.

Jim and Ron also flew the airplane to an antique aircraft show in Casa Grande on a Friday afternoon. A storm front arrived on Saturday morning, delivering wind and rain for the whole weekend. The *City of Yuma* won the Best Aeronca at Show award. The wind continued all weekend, so a decision was made to leave the airplane at Casa Grande until the weather cleared, which was two days later.

On April 11, 2000, Jim flew the airplane out to Roll, landing near the Mohawk Valley School, where students were waiting to see the airplane and hear stories from Jim, Bob Woodhouse, and Bob's sister, Shirley Murdock. The students were attentive and had interesting questions. They were excited about seeing the airplane and getting to sit in the seats and imagine two men living in those close quarters for *almost seven weeks*. They wrote many thank-you notes after such an interesting day.

Mohawk Valley School students observing the *City of Yuma* at their school in Roll, April 11, 2003.

To make sure that the airplane would be available for these events, Jim checked out Mike Taylor, a certified flight instructor, who in turn would certify other pilots such as Paul Rachels to fly these missions. The last flight to an air show was in 2003 in Parker, Arizona, where a mid-air collision occurred between a WWII navy F6F Hellcat and a civilian aircraft. Subsequently, a decision was made not to fly the airplane again. The *City of Yuma* was featured in *Air Classics* magazine as a result of the visit to Parker.

In 2007 Horace Griffen was contacted by David Majure, executive producer for Arizona State University's KAET channel 8. David wanted to interview Horace about his experience as a flight instructor for British pilots at Falcon Field in Scottsdale during WWII. During David's visit to Horace's home in Casa Grande, he noticed pictures of the *City of Yuma* airplane hanging on the wall and asked about the story behind it. Horace was glad to talk about it. After hearing the story, David decided to produce a feature story about the *City of Yuma* flight and to include it in *The Arizona History Collection of Arizona Stories, Season III*, a DVD of short stories about some of the state's most fascinating people and historically significant places and events.

David and his crew came to Yuma in early 2008 to interview people, collect data, and take photos of MCAS Yuma, the *City of Yuma* airplane, and the refueling car. The program was first aired on KAET on October 28, 2008. After the program aired, a number of people called in claiming to have the original wooden propeller that was used during the flight. They were in error, however, because the airplane was manufactured with an aluminum propeller.

CHAPTER FIVE

OLD-TIMERS REMEMBER THOSE FORTY-SEVEN DAYS

Through the years, people of Yuma have kept the 1949 endurance flight of the *City of Yuma* alive and well in their hearts.

It was especially so for Horace Griffen. It has been one of his most favorite subjects of conversation, and he has kept in touch with just about everyone who was involved in the flight.

Evening refueling run. Woody is being congratulated by a visiting dignitary. Photo by Emil Eger.

TIME MARCHES ON

Several of the people who were most involved in the flight have passed away and are sorely missed by those who remain, especially as the sixtieth anniversary approaches.

Paul Burch was killed in a tragic accident at the Yuma County Airport in December of 1979. The pilot of a military jet, an A-4, ejected on takeoff when the airplane lost directional control. He didn't shut the engine down, and the aircraft continued, under full power and unattended. It was headed northeast, then veered about 30 degrees toward the north and crashed into the hangar where Paul was in his shop. He was killed instantly, and the pilot was found walking on the runway. Paul Burch was a prominent figure in aviation history in Yuma. In addition to being an aircraft mechanic at Marsh Airport for many years and then having his own business, Burch Aviation, he was a major founder and the first president of the airport authority. He was often referred to as a "super mechanic."

Charlie Gilpin's death in December 1985 was a shock—sudden and unexpected. The cause was toxemia resulting from a gall bladder infection. He had retired as general manager of Gilpin's Construction Co., Inc. in 1977, turning the business over to Don Riley, his daughter Jeffie's husband. Charlie did this in order to be able to spend more time with his wife, Julie, who had contracted cancer the previous year. Julie passed away on January 1, 1978. Charlie continued to own the business and remained chairman of the board, but he didn't work there. He married Ann, and they traveled extensively for several years before his untimely death.

Bernie Pensky died of cancer in July of 1990. He and Woody Jongeward were next-door neighbors in their businesses. Bernie's son, Perry, said that Woody probably asked Bernie about having Penn Signs paint all the signs on the *City of Yuma* and on the refueling car and maybe even about serving on the morning refueling crew. Griff referred to Bernie as being "the tall one on the morning crew." Bernie and Bob Hodge were good friends, dating from their military pilot days at the air base. Perry mentioned that a lot of Yuma businessmen had been stationed at the air base and came back to Yuma after they got out of the service because they liked the town so well.

Perry also said that, when he was young and into sand rails and motorcycles, Bernie worried because those things were "dangerous." Perry said, "I said to him, 'When you were my age, you were standing up in a speeding convertible, handing cans full of gasoline to some guys in an airplane that was right there beside you, and you think what I'm doing is *dangerous*?'"

Bob Hodge also died of cancer in January of 1995. He went to Scripps in La Jolla in 1994 and was diagnosed with "a very fast-acting terminal cancer in the top of his head and in his lungs," his son, Mike, said. He went to Tucson for a second opinion and was told the same thing. The prognosis was that he probably only had four to six months to live. "He didn't whimper on the way out," Mike said. "He was very courageous and never lost track of who he was."

Mike said that when his father became frail, he didn't want other people to see him. He wanted them to remember him the way he had been before. Mike also said that Yuma has changed so rapidly and that most people don't remember those old-timers like Bob Woodhouse, Woody Jongeward, Charlie Gilpin, and Bernie Pensky. "They were pioneers, explorers, adventurers; they tested the envelopes in their own ways."

There are others, too numerous to mention, but individually missed by those who worked and played with them.

THIS WAS A BIG EVENT

The endurance flight of 1949 was one of the most exciting and interesting things ever to happen in this corner of Arizona, and it had a major effect on the economy and the fortunes of those who settled and invested in the area. A sudden bright idea grasped, pursued, and effectively carried out made a difference.

Old-timers enjoy reminiscing about the days when the *City of Yuma* held their attention and Bob and Woody were the heroes of the day. The spirit of the community is a thing to be remembered with some sentiment and appreciation. Refueling was the high point of the day for everybody, including the many citizens not directly responsible for any aspect of the flight. The exchange of gas, oil, and food between the car and the airplane never failed to excite the expectant crowds at the airport. The evening refuelings became the place to be. The press always reminded Yumans that they were welcome, but that they must stay clear of the runways. The early-morning runs were not as popular as a spectator sport; but the wives, Berta and Betty, were out there for every refueling run, morning as well as evening. Griff said, "There wasn't one run made, during the entire flight, without either Berta or Betty"—and they both had full-time jobs. One morning in the early stages of the flight, the wives started handing fuel cans up to the pilots when someone didn't show up on time. After that, they were "officially adopted" by the morning refueling crew, and they took an active part. Sometimes they were boosted up by a couple of members of the ground crew to within "smooching distance" of their husbands. Pictures of that activity made front pages of newspapers and some newsreels. In a letter handed down to his parents, Bob wrote of the wives: "They are always out there and all smiles, even at the early-morning refueling. I think it's harder on them than it is on us. We're getting more sleep than they are, by far."

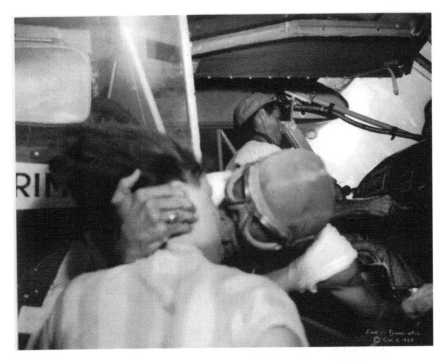

October 6, 1949. Bob and Berta sharing a high-speed kiss the day after the existing world's record of 1,008 hours was broken. Photo by Emil Eger.

There was an incident that livened things up a bit during one of the refueling runs, and Bob told how it happened. "On one occasion 'Big Bob Hodge,' who was 6 feet, 7 inches tall and weighed about 275 pounds, was in the refueling car, and somebody else was handing us a gas can. Well, Hodge reached up and grabbed the strut to try to stabilize the airplane. We couldn't really tell where that force was coming from, but all of a sudden the airplane was tilting to the right. So what did I do? Well, I gave it a little more left aileron. And what did Hodge do? He pulled it down more. I'm thinkin' that the airplane is going haywire somehow. Well, he finally got all of it he needed, and he turned it loose. So then the airplane went 'Whoom!' with the right wing high. Ol' Hodge was probably holdin' a hundred pounds of weight down, and I'd been tryin' to overcome it." Several people have mentioned that Bob Hodge lifted those gas cans up as easily as if they were empty, "never mind the wind resistance as the car and airplane sped down the runway."

Probably the question most often asked is, "How did you handle your bathroom routine?" Bob said, "Well, Berta went down to Imperial Hardware and bought an aluminum pot with handles on each side. Somebody came up with some insulated bags that were made out of two layers of a kind of asphalt-type stuff with chopped-up paper in between the layers. At that time you couldn't just go buy plastic bags. These were waterproof and insulated, and they had a little wire or somethin' that you twisted around the top. That bag would just fit in the pot and the edges would turn down a little ways. So whenever you got whatever you wanted in that pot, then you'd pull it up and twist that little wire around the top and then we'd fly over to California and throw it out, 'cause we had heard that they needed the water over there."

Air-to-air shot showing Bob drying off after taking a sponge bath. Photo by Rod Daley.

One day Griff told Bob over the radio that a load of new Buicks had come in, and he said, "You guys ought to fly over and take a look at them and pick one out to buy when you land." Bob said, "Well, bring them out to the airport for us to take a look at, and we'll make a deposit on one of those suckers!"

HAIR REMOVAL MANIFESTO

The *Yuma Daily Sun* had an amusing article on September 13, 1949. "Today marked the twentieth day in the air for endurance fliers Bob Woodhouse and Woody Jongeward and also instituted 'The Big Shave.' True to his word, state Junior Chamber of Commerce president Ray Smucker fulfilled his promise this morning to rid his scalp of its hairy covering. Sixteen men and five lariat ropes finally subdued the Herculean head of radio station KYUM so that Cecil Huling of the Sunshine Barber Shop could do the honors. Following in the footsteps of his idol, Samson, Smucker became meek as a kitten as soon as his locks dissolved partnership with his noggin.

"Getting back a little closer to what actually happened, Woodhouse and Jongeward, after a slight conference of two weeks on the subject, sent down word that they would settle for a half inch of hair to be left. As soon as the decision was handed down, a loud cheer went up from the ranks of the Jaycees on the ground.

"This morning as usual Smucker was making his regular morning blowcast when the door flew open and in walked Yuma Jaycee prexy Charlie Gilpin and Barber Cecil Huling. Without so much as a goodbye phone call to his wife, Smucker allowed the towel and apron to be fastened in place, the clippers plugged in, and his tresses removed while he continued his work at the microphone.

"Each day hereafter, Woodhouse and Jongeward will fill out one 'Big Shave' ticket which entitles the person whose name is enclosed to one free skinning at The Sunshine Barber Shop. The bearer must have the ticket honored by 10:00 AM. All recipients of 'The Big Shave' tickets who take their turns peaceably will be allowed a half inch of hair. God help the stubborn— who will be Number Two? Read the next exciting episode in tomorrow's *Sun*."

WHAT CAN WE DO TODAY?

Sometimes the playful refueling crew had a surprise dreamed up for the pilots. Suggestive reading materials were not unheard of, and on one occasion the pilots' gift of the day was a new exercise pad made up of several dozen realistic-looking "falsies" of all sizes and shapes.

Another time, according to the *Yuma Daily Sun*, a well-meaning refueling crew member included two beers with the usual orange juice and milk in an ice chest that was handed up to the pilots. They couldn't drink beer, so Woody opened both cans and returned the brew to the refueling crew on the next pass.

The pilots devised ways in which to amuse themselves. Bob described one of their little schemes that brought a reaction from a major sponsor. "Sometimes we'd fly over the dump, which was down by the river in those days, and we'd pick out a target to bomb with oil cans. But then the guys that were given' us the oil, Union Oil Company, decided that all of a sudden the oil consumption on the airplane had gone up considerably. We were usin' two or three quarts more each day than we had been usin'. Well, we told 'em, 'You know, with empty oil cans, you throw one of them out, and it just goes *pfffffft*, and you can't hit anything with 'em, so we're usin' full ones.' So they sent up some grapefruit for us to do our bombin' with."

On another occasion, Bob and Woody told about an amusing little trick that they played on one of the refueling crews. The fliers asked the morning refueling crew to help them conduct their ruse. They sent a note down asking the group to go to the junkyard and find the nastiest, greasiest old carburetor that they could and put it in a cottonseed sack. The men were able to get an old carburetor from an airplane, and they passed it up to the pilots the next morning. During the evening refueling, they said to the crew, "We've got something here that we have to get fixed right away, so take this to Paul and get it fixed as soon as possible," and they handed them the old wrapped-up carburetor.

Some people remember that Woody asked for a first-aid kit one morning, "including some snakebite medicine." He said that Bob had been bitten by a rattlesnake. The truth was that Bob had a recurring dream in which he came upon a coiled rattlesnake and he kept trying to get away from it. His family members knew what it was like to be near him when he was having a nightmare, and all felt sympathy for Woody, stuck with him in that three-foot-wide cabin. There was also a question of the real need for "snakebite medicine."

The cook at the Valley Café during those years was Henry Casares who lived in Yuma until his death in July 2009. He remembered seeing the *City of Yuma* flying over all the time and the excitement about it. He knew just about everybody in town, as the Valley Café was "the place to see and be seen." Henry worked the 5:00 P.M. to 1:00 A.M. shift and remembers seeing the airplane flying around Yuma in the early morning hours. He stated that he showed his daughters the airplane and told them that they were "looking at history and that is when things became meaningful." He offered as an analogy that you can read about the Grand Canyon all you want, but when you actually go look at it and it takes your breath away, you truly understand what a marvel it is.

Then there was the time that the pilots "dropped the watch," or more accurately, "the watches." Everett Self owned The Sweet Shop in Self's Enterprise Building in Somerton. He had a soda fountain, a newsstand, a bus station, and even a jewelry department and watch repair business. That was "the in place" in Somerton. Charles Phillips was the watch repairman. Everett and Charles asked if the pilots would drop two Wyler shockproof watches from an altitude of one thousand feet onto the concrete runway at the airport to prove and advertise that they were shockproof. The plan was agreed upon and Charlie Gilpin placed an empty gas can on the runway as a target. He told the pilots that, if they came within six feet of the can, the watches would be theirs. Paul Dawson of KYUM helped with the publicity, but he had been dubious about the claim and asked the editor of the *Somerton Star* newspaper to bring along a broom and a dustpan to sweep up the pieces. About five hundred spectators attended a refueling when the watches were dropped with red, white, and blue streamers attached to them with adhesive tape. The whisk broom and dustpan were not needed, as the second hands on both watches were moving along normally. There were several "official judges" of the condition of the watches, which were also inspected by about fifty spectators. Charlie Gilpin asked the pilots whether they wanted the watches that they had dropped or new ones. Everett said, "They enthusiastically voted on those that they had helped to prove were shockproof."

At Horace Griffen's request, Bob Hodge and Jeffie Gilpin Riley organized the celebration of the fortieth anniversary of that big day in 1949. Griff served as master of ceremonies at a Rotary meeting at lunchtime on October 10, 1989, and then at the dinner at Chretin's in the evening. He introduced all of those in attendance and when he came to Bob and Pauline Hodge, he said, "Bob was chosen for the refueling crew for an obvious reason. In those days he was taller than he was wide."

Later, when people were telling stories of the days of the flight, Bob Hodge said, "One of my favorite stories is about Bobby and Woody. They were up in the air. We had a hamburger spot downtown, and there was a girl down there who was built like you-know-what—Genola Gray. So Bertie and Betty were in the convertible with me, and we went down to get a hamburger, but the boys didn't know that the girls were in the car. They said on the radio, 'Where you goin'?' and I said, 'We're going down to get a hamburger.' They said, 'Oh, is Genola workin'?' And I said, 'I don't know, I'm gonna find out.' So we got there, and they said, 'Genola?' So I asked her, 'Do you want to speak to the boys?' And she said, 'Sure. Hi, Bobby! Hi, Woody!' They said, 'Oh, hi, Genola!' So they chatted back and forth, and Bertie and Betty and I were eatin' our food, and we got all through, and the boys said that they wanted to speak to Genola again. So they said, 'Genola, when we get back down, the first thing we're gonna do is come down and get a hamburger and a malted milk.' I said, 'Is that right? *The very first thing?*' They said, 'Yeah!' I said, 'Well, I've got to leave you guys, but there's one more thing I want to do,' and I handed the microphone to Betty and she said, 'Good night, Woody,' and she handed the mike to Bertie, and she said, 'Good night, Bob!'—There was total silence!"

SIDE TRIPS

The airplane droned around Yuma, ventured into California, and paid Phoenix a visit on the occasion of a parade honoring Jacque Mercer, who brought the Miss America crown home to Arizona and to her hometown of Phoenix. The endurance airplane flew over the parade and then circled the state capitol building as Miss America received the official greetings of her home state.

According to the *Sun*, on the twenty-second day of the flight, the pilots acted as messenger boys for the Yuma and Phoenix Rotary Clubs.. Rotary was sponsoring an appearance of Horace Heidt with his show in both cities. When the Phoenix organization ran short of publicity posters advertising the Horace Heidt Show, the fliers were approached about running an errand for the Phoenix Rotarians. They complied and were scheduled to head their light plane in the direction of the capitol city just as soon as permission had been obtained for them to drop the bundles at Sky Harbor Airport. An excellent photo captured the moment when the package was dropped.

The *City of Yuma* delivering a package for the Horace Heidt show in Phoenix,
September 15, 1949.

That was the same day that a 4:00 A.M. refueling was added to the
schedule, as described in the second chapter.

The pilots' travels included four trips to Phoenix, and on other days, they
flew to Tempe or Chandler, Winslow, Coolidge, Tucson, or Casa Grande. An
article in the *Yuma Daily Sun* indicated that one of their favorite tours was to
Los Angeles and along the coast from there to San Diego, "checking out the
beaches."

On one occasion, the pilots suddenly found that they had flown far away
from their usual territory. Bob related the story at a modern-day meeting.

WAKE UP! WHERE ARE WE?

"One night, Woody woke me up, and he was lookin' around, kinda scared-
lookin', and he said, 'Bob! What are those lights there?'

"I said, 'I don't know. Why?'

"He said, 'Well, I've been asleep!'

"And you could sleep in that airplane. I had gone to sleep when I was flyin', and he'd gone to sleep before. He might have slept quite a while that time; but if you flew maybe three or four minutes, the airplane would usually begin to drift off one way or the other, and the engine would speed up, 'cause, you know, it had a fixed-pitch propeller, so the sound would change, and you'd wake up. So, I'm lookin' around, and I'm thinkin'—you know, I can't see Mexicali, and I can't see Yuma.

"I said, 'Well, whatever town that is, it's back behind us, so I'd suggest we turn around and go back there and see what it is!'

"Well, it took us almost an hour gettin' back there. We figured we were the other side of Puertecitos, maybe Gonzaga," two Baja fishing villages on the Gulf of California, some distance "south of the border."

A Yuma veteran was a patient at Fort Whipple Veterans' Hospital at Prescott. He knew that the pilots traveled around, and he wondered if they might come and fly over the hospital so that he could see them. They honored that request, flying over the hospital at an altitude of about 1,500 feet on September 28.

THE PARTY BEGINS

September 28 was also the day that the pilots completed five weeks in the air. With only another week to go before breaking the record, the local news was full of plans for a "reception" as the pilots flew low over the runway. Yumans were advised just where to line up their cars, and the Jaycees suggested that each person take a white tea towel or something white to wave at the pilots. The Yuma Bus Company provided free rides to and from the airport for the refueling that evening and on other occasions. Yumans were advised that they could stop the bus at any point by waving a white tea towel. Bob and Woody were surprised to see a crowd, estimated at five thousand people, gathered at the airport, whereupon they received their salute of white tea towels. Such demonstrations gave them the needed boost for the long hours of living in a small space, approximately six feet by four and a half feet, for almost seven weeks.

Another highlight of that event was the deputizing of the fliers by Sheriff Jack Beard. The official cards were sent up to the pilots during the evening refueling. Also two new blankets were handed up to the pilots. They were donated by Horace Porter of The United, a store in downtown Yuma.

The *Yuma Daily Sun* article on that day stated, "Folks attending the refueling will probably notice a change in the title of the make of the pickup which is used for hauling the gas cans and oil to the airport. On the tailgate of the truck, the title did read 'Dodge,' but now reads, 'Hodge.' The truck and the fuel to keep the very important vehicle going were donated by Bob Hodge, General Petroleum distributor in Yuma. Hodge is also on the board of directors of the Yuma Junior Chamber of Commerce and a member of the evening refueling crew." (At one time, the truck for that purpose was provided by Union Oil Company, as noted elsewhere. Apparently that responsibility changed at some point during the flight.)

On September 22, the twenty-ninth day of the flight, the Jaycees sold coffee and sandwiches at the airport. The Swift Company exhibited a six-foot-long hot dog in the window of the L & R Market that day and said that they would make sandwiches from the meat in that display and sell them at the airport that evening. They also made coffee and sold it, donating the proceeds to the Jaycees, who used the funds to help defray expenses associated with the flight. The sandwiches sold for ten cents apiece and the coffee for a nickel! The article in the *Sun* hinted, "There just might be some sort of added entertainment thrown in on the deal, for attending flight boosters."

THE FAT LADY STARTS TO SING

At one point during the second attempt, the *Yuma Daily Sun* carried this story:

> "Endurance Fliers Hear Jaycee Song. Never to be outdone on any count, the Yuma Junior Chamber of Commerce is building up more momentum every day in putting over its endurance flight. When pilots Bob Woodhouse and Woody Jongeward brought their light ship down from the blue this morning to refuel, they were greeted over the radio with a song. While the fliers circled the field prior to swooping down to pick up fuel and supplies, the ground-crewmen sprang the latest Jaycee surprise: a song, composed principally by Bob Hodge. The words are sung to the tune of 'McNamara's Band.'
>
> 'Here are the words:
>
> 'Oh we've got a couple of pilots of whom we're mighty proud.

We're going to shout their praises and we'll shout them clear and loud.
Their names are Woodhouse and Jongeward and the two of them can't be beat,
And they'll be leading the whole parade when they turn on the heat.
Give 'em a ship that they can fly, Now watch these boys, they're mighty sly;
If the ship don't quit, it's do or die and we'll watch the old endurance record go bye-bye.'

"Still another song about the refueling:

'Here comes a man with a can in his hand,
He's got gasoline in that can—Honey, Baby mine.
Gasoline in that can is yours,
Hurry, Hurry, open your doors—Honey, Baby mine.
Lean 'way out, reach 'way down,
Be damn sure you don't touch the ground—Honey, Baby mine.
Hurry, hurry, get in a rush.
We're almost clear down to the brush—Honey, Baby mine.
Jongeward, hurry and get that stuff.
We're not taking any of your guff—Honey, Baby mine.'

"And a poem written by Lucille Foos.

'High over Yuma by day and night
Are happening many things
And every Yuman stands and cheers
At a flash of silver wings.
Why does everyone stand with bated breath
And maybe breathe a prayer?
It's something great, haven't you heard?
Yuma is in the air.
Two men of Yuma have gone aloft
To prove by actual test
That no matter how good flying weather is,
In Yuma, it's always best.
So ride on Knights of the air,
May your engine never fail,
But waft you gently through the sky
Till you hit the homeward trail.

You're not alone as you wing your way
Up there in the Heavenly blue,
But every Yuman's thoughts and prayers
Are riding there with you.
Think of California's face when you've won the race
As you take your needed rest.
Bring that record down to your home town,
Yuma, the star of the West.'"

Ironically, just a few minutes before that record was broken, someone landed at the airport in an Aeronca Sedan, exactly the same kind and color of airplane as the *City of Yuma*. It was dark enough that the absence of signs and slogans wasn't easily seen. A few Yumans almost had heart failure. That pilot could hardly believe the sensation that he had created.

FLIGHT TO CHICAGO

After the forty-seven-day flight, interest continued to be evident around the country. The endurance fliers flew the *City of Yuma* to Chicago where they rode a float with the airplane along Michigan Avenue for the National Jaycee Convention in 1950. Betty and Berta said, "Not without us!"; and they accompanied their husbands on that trip.

Bob's parents, Harold and Ethelind Woodhouse, and his sister, Shirley, made that same trip, flying along beside the endurance fliers and their wives in another airplane. A former neighbor, George Foelsch, had moved from Roll to his home state of Wisconsin; and he said to the Woodhouses, "If you'll fly my Stinson Voyager from Roll back here to Wisconsin, I'll pay your airline fares back to Arizona." Shirley was just home from college in Colorado, and she was delighted to go along, to visit relatives in Wisconsin and then attend the Jaycee Convention in Chicago and see the *City of Yuma* and the pilots on a float in a big city parade.

As the Arizonans were flying over Kansas, Betty Jongeward said, "Boy! If you were going to buy a farm in this part of the country, you'd have to buy a used one, wouldn't you?" She wasn't accustomed to seeing every acre of land under cultivation.

MODEL AIRPLANES CAN DO ENDURANCE FLIGHTS, TOO

A model airplane was built as an exact replica of the *City of Yuma* with all the same signs and slogans, but with a wingspan of six feet. It was one-sixth the size of the original record-holding Aeronca. Yumans Thurman Hart and his son, Billy, were the "co-pilots" who flew the model on a hundred-foot line, controlled from a jeep driven by Herschel Wright. The Jaycees sponsored a second endurance flight with the model, which they called the *City of Yuma, Jr.*, setting a record for model airplanes, on October 10, 1952, the third anniversary of the record set by its "big brother."

Model airplane, the *City of Yuma, Jr.* (1/6 scale), built by Bob McFarlane.

Young "Billy" Hart grew up and became an elementary school principal. He sent to the authors an amusing saga of the endurance flight of the *City of Yuma, Jr.*, which read as follows:

"For what it's worth, here is a little more history on the bird:

"Bob MacFarlane built the airplane and then recruited Dad and me to fly it for him. I was the Arizona junior state model champion at the time and was supposed to know how to fly the thing! We test flew it at Marsh Airport, down by the river, and promptly tore the bird up! Dad helped rebuild the thing, removing the wing warp and bringing the balance way forward. He also incorporated two fuel tanks in the wings in order to keep the weight on the center of gravity.

"A model on control lines flies in a continual circle with the pilot, who controls pitch only, standing in the center. Following the repairs, the bird flew like a dream, but was fast. She flew at sixty to seventy miles an hour—we had no throttle, of course!—and even on one-hundred-foot control lines the bird would be impossible to catch and refuel in mid air.

"I think it was Paul Burch—super-mechanic at Marsh and second dad to me—who came up with the idea of flying the bird from a moving jeep. We could travel in almost a straight line, giving our brave refueling crew in a pickup the opportunity to catch the plane and feed it.

Model airplane, the *City of Yuma, Jr.*, during its own endurance flight, October 10, 1952.

"We flew several practice flights at the county airport, and things went well. On the morning of October 10, 1952, we took off to try for the record. I was given the honor of being the first pilot, and I remember the sudden feeling of fear in trying to get the bird off the ground. It seems that we never made a practice flight with full fuel tanks, and the bird weighed a ton! We lumbered into the air and the resulting pull on the control lines about took my young arm off! It was definitely time for the second pilot (Dad) to fly this thing!

"Russ Phillips solved the problem of heavy pull on the control lines by driving the jeep in as straight a line as possible, making a very wide 180-degree turn and traveling back. Also, as the fuel burned off, it became lighter and it was easier to fly.

"Refueling was another matter. I was flying when Dad decided it was time to feed the bird. Russ drove as straight as possible and the wild-eyed crew in the pickup came thundering after us—in one of the flight photos you can see a long plastic tube trailing from the bird. The plan was for the guys in the pickup to grab the end of the tube, push it on a fitting screwed into a two-gallon tank of gas-and-oil mixture, and then pump like crazy on a tire pump to pressurize the tank, which would move the fuel up the line and into the tanks. When finished, they were supposed to pull the plastic tube off the pressurized tank and we were free to go—another Paul Burch idea, I think!—This was all great but after we finally matched a moving jeep, a moving airplane and a moving pickup, we forgot about one thing—the wind!

"To make a long story much shorter, the pickup came right up under the bird and we were caught in the wind breaking over the cab, due to a head wind we were fighting. The airplane was swept over the cab and down into the bed, flying—I swear—less than two feet behind the back window! The guys in the pickup bed—the refueling crew—were all lying on their backs trying to become as small as possible, and all the while my prop turning at about twelve thousand RPM was inches over their heads! At that moment I became the world's first gray-haired kid.

"Dad hollered at me that I was about to kill our fuel crew, as if I needed a reminder, and I pulled full back pressure on the control handle. As we broke out and climbed off above the pickup, one of the crew grabbed the plastic tube and pulled us backward! This created a second set of gray hairs. After a great tug-of-war we had fuel and were free again. I was happy to let Dad fly for a long time afterward.

"Dad handed off to me again and shortly after that I heard the engine stumble for the first time. Russ tightened up the circle he was driving to keep tension on the control lines and Dad told me to stay with it. It didn't take a genius to know that our flight was in big trouble. Our faithful Anderson Spitfire engine rapidly lost power and then simply quit. With a lump in my throat the size of a basketball I let her glide to slow down and then made one of the best landings of my life—then and now. With mixed emotions we all shook hands and the rest is history."

—Bill Hart

The *Yuma Daily Sun* featured articles with accompanying photographs in advance of the flight of the *City of Yuma, Jr.* in its attempt to establish a world's endurance flight record for model airplanes. The October 10, 1952, issue of the *Sun* displayed a headline that read, "Model Plane Stays Up One Hour, Ten Minutes." The article explained, "Ignition trouble brought the Jaycees' model airplane, the *City of Yuma, Jr.*, down after one hour, ten minutes and forty-seven seconds, but the Jaycees were claiming the world's record in spite of the short run."

The article stated that Herschel Wright, driving the jeep, was able to establish contact with the model for four minutes while the crew of Odell Stafford and Harry Dye managed to get some gasoline into the airplane. Official timers for the model airplane flight were Dr. P. A. Birdick and "watch owners" Glenn Gartland and Gene Kornfeld, as the *Sun* referred to two prominent jewelry store proprietors of that era. The airplane had a three-quart fuel capacity, and the crew had hoped to keep it in flight for five hours; but oil got on the points of the motor and forced the flight to end. The *City of Yuma, Jr.* hung in the museum at the Yuma Territorial Prison for a number of years; but the prison was remodeled, and the whereabouts of the model have been unknown since that time.

THE RECORD IS BROKEN

Ten years after their endurance flight, Bob and Woody were participants on *I've Got a Secret,* Garry Moore's popular national television show. They flew to New York for the show, which was arranged by the indomitable Ray Smucker, and the panel of contestants failed to guess their secret. As a result of that show, the Hacienda Hotel in Las Vegas sponsored a flight that broke the Yuma record.

Then, on April 27, 1991, the two pilots, Robert Woodhouse and Woodrow Jongeward, were inducted into the *Arizona Aviation Hall of Fame* at the Pima Air Museum near Tucson at its second annual induction ceremony. The only four prior honorees were Frank Luke, Jr., Walter Douglas, Jr., Barry Goldwater, and Frank Borman. The endurance fliers' plaque states in part: "A support team of six hundred people was required for this highly-coordinated enterprise which was a punishing test of both men and machine."

The White House Millennium Council designated the city of Yuma, Arizona, as a millennium community with a certificate signed by President Bill Clinton. That certificate and a letter from the White House offering congratulations for being selected were received by the mayor's office on September 20, 1999.

AN UPDATE REGARDING THE MAJOR PLAYERS:

BOB

Bob had to slow down a little as he approached the age of eighty. He was finally feeling those years after an active life as a farmer and an avid outdoorsman. He had a Harley and often went on trips with a much younger crowd, always enjoying himself with the group, and they enjoyed him. He liked to go camping and hunting, especially for elk and deer but also rabbits and other small game.

He and Berta had a home at the Country Club at Show Low, Arizona, and they spent a great deal of time there to escape the desert's summer heat. One day he took a bad fall, down a brick staircase, and suffered severe damage to his head. He was taken by Air Evac helicopter from Show Low to the Barrow Neurological Center in Phoenix, and that marked a major step in his downhill progress. He still enjoyed having company and visiting with people, but on the night of December 23, 2003, after having a relaxing massage, he died peacefully in his sleep.

The *Yuma Sun* ran an article, well written by Pam Smith, with the headline of that section reading, "Yuma Mourns Loss of Record-Setting Pilot" and an article titled "Losing a Legend" after the memorial service and tributes at the cemetery; both articles showed several pictures.

Bob had lived in Roll, Arizona, about fifty miles east of Yuma, since the age of two, and having been in business as a farmer and serving on several boards for many years, he was widely known, aside from his participation in the endurance flight. A memorial service was held at the Mohawk Valley School in Roll, officiated by Cecil Pratt, pastor of the Mohawk Valley Presbyterian Church. There were approximately 350 people in attendance, many having driven out from Yuma. A slide show was presented, and several people expressed heartfelt special memories.

Mike Taylor flew the *City of Yuma* from Yuma, with John Youkey as his "crew," and parked it in front of the school, where everyone appreciated seeing it. Then when the hearse and others were driving to Yuma after the service, Mike and John flew past the procession, dipping one wing and then the other in a well-known salute. That was a memorable moment for everyone who observed it.

At the cemetery, just after the little graveside ceremony was completed for Bob, a most touching aerial salute was made with the *City of Yuma* and four other private airplanes flying over the scene in formation and saluting the group with the usual dipping of wings. Accompanying Mike Taylor in the endurance airplane was his father, Jack Taylor. In the formation of four airplanes were Paul Rachels, flying a Cessna 170B with Neil Ruth as his "crew"; Ed Justice, flying a Cessna 175 with Fred Acosta; Billy Jessup flying a Cessna 170 with Ed Whitehead; and Jim Ehrhart flying a Cessna 140. It was a dramatic finale to the ceremony and a special moment to be long remembered by all who were there. Someone said that it was like something choreographed in a movie. Several men mentioned that there was probably not a dry eye in the whole crowd.

The *City of Yuma* in "missing man formation" at conclusion of graveside services for Bob Woodhouse, December 27, 2003.

Following the service, many returned to the Mohawk Valley School for a barbecue and fellowship, finishing the celebration of Bob's life in a manner that he would have appreciated.

(Note: In 2008 Mike Taylor suffered a heart attack and, subsequently, a stroke. At the time of this writing, he is progressing in his recovery.)

WOODY

When Woody became the pilot for the endurance flight project, he left his brother, Howard, in charge of their business, Jongeward Electric, which they had established just three years earlier, in 1946.

After the flight, exactly one year from the date that he and Bob took off for their successful attempt at the endurance flight record, Woody and Betty's daughter, Karen, was born. That was August 24, 1950. They continued to live in Yuma for many years. In 1984 they purchased a home in Shell Beach, California, which they rented out for about two years. Then, in 1986, they sold their home in Yuma and moved to their new home in Shell Beach. Shortly before that time, they had sold their business to a company in Phoenix.

In August of 2003, Betty was in poor health, and they sold their home in Shell Beach and moved to the San Diego area to be near their daughter, Karen, and her husband, Bob Tanner. They bought a condo there. Betty passed away a few months later, in December of 2003.

Woody turned ninety-one in April of 2009, and he still lives alone in the condo. Karen and Bob live near there, and Karen goes to see him every afternoon, at least. Woody is still able to travel by commercial airline, sometimes alone, to visit his son in Virginia, and there are various little trips that he still hopes to make.

HORACE GRIFFEN

In the late 1960s, Griff and Jackie moved to Durango, Colorado. He sold the Buick dealership and became a New York Life Insurance Company agent. He and Jackie had an agency in Durango for a number of years. They retired and enjoyed traveling around the country and then had a winter home in Yuma for a while. They lived in Durango until 2001, when they decided to move to Casa Grande, Arizona, where their son, Kent, and his wife, Anne, live. They built a nice home on the edge of a golf course there, and then Jackie was stricken with lung cancer. She passed away in March of 2004. Griff lives there and is still active and enjoying life at age eighty-eight.

Griff has always loved to tell the story of the endurance flight to people whom he meets. He sparks their interest so that they want a copy of *The Longest Flight*, and then he orders more and more books. He is still, to this day, frequently asked to be the guest speaker at service club events or occasions associated with aviation, to tell about the flight. Having been a flight instructor during WWII, he remains in contact with some of those associates.

CHUCK MABERY

Chuck was raised in Yuma and lived there until 1958 when he and his family moved to Prescott, Arizona. Two years later they moved to Cottonwood, Arizona. In October of 1994, he and his family opened The Blazin' M Barbeque and Show, featuring a chuck wagon supper and live Western stage show. They built a unique little antique western village with an Old Tyme Photo Studio, where one can dress up in costumes of the 1880s. There are several old-fashioned shops and a little "Wood 'n' West" gallery with hand-carved, historical scenes with small moving figures. It's a "one-of-a-kind-in-the-world" museum. A big, delicious meal is served, followed by an entertaining and amusing show with several excellent musicians—all in a Western theme.

Chuck retired from the ownership of the Blazin' M on December 31, 2008, and turned the operation over to his family. Shortly after that, in January of 2009, his wife, Lucreta, passed away.

GEORGE MURDOCK

George was raised in Alabama but settled in Yuma after serving in the army in Alaska during World War II. He worked for Horace Griffen, at Griffen Buick, as a mechanic and then as service manager. In 1951 he and Shirley Woodhouse married; and then in 1954, they moved to Roll and have been farming there on the farm where Shirley's parents settled as pioneers in 1925. They raised their four children there; and now their two sons, Kenny and Jimmy, are partners with George in Murdock Farms and have raised their own families in Roll.

George is eighty-two years old at the time of this writing and is still active and in good health, and Shirley is also. One of George's hobbies is restoring old cars, and he has a collection of those.

Shirley Woodhouse Murdock and James A. Gillaspie

* * * * * * * * * * * * *

THE POWER OF PEOPLE WORKING TOGETHER

In the future, scholars will look back at Yuma's progress through the twentieth century, and they will note that the most significant of many turning points in Yuma's march to success occurred in 1949 with the Longest Flight.

The manner in which the people of Yuma pulled together to make this happen and take Yuma forward was a high point that may never be equaled again. One fact stands out: Yuma in 1949 was at the crossroads of mediocrity and success, and through the efforts of those six hundred volunteers, the path to success was made available. To honor those of the past who made this possible, the *City of Yuma* story was recently selected to be Yuma's entry to the White House Millennium Program, "Honor the Past—Imagine the Future." Judy Spencer provided the required information to Mike Shelton, assistant city administrator, who in turn coupled this information with a proclamation from Mayor Young and sent it to Washington, D.C. These items will become a part of the White House Project Web site, making t*he City of Yuma*'s Longest Flight known to the world once again. The *City of Yuma* will live forever.

CHAPTER SIX

FUTURE HOME OF THE *CITY OF YUMA* AIRPLANE

Fate sometimes deals an unexpected hand. As stated in chapter three, the eventual goal for the *City of Yuma* airplane was to get it placed in a museum or other venue in Yuma for future generations to enjoy. That easily stated goal has been difficult to accomplish for a number of reasons, but the effort continues.

STILL LOOKING

In December 1999, Ron and Jim and other Jaycee Foundation members were invited to attend a meeting of the Yuma Crossing National Heritage Area Corporation, which was working to improve the historical downtown and riverfront areas of Yuma. Charles Flynn briefed the group concerning the goals of the Foundation. He further stated that, in his opinion, the flight of the *City of Yuma* was one of Yuma's most historic accomplishments. He also stated that, because of strong public sentiment, the proposed welcome center to be located at Fifth Avenue and the Colorado River west of the Arizona inspection station could serve as the new home for the airplane. The welcome center, designed to be a gateway to Yuma and the state of Arizona, is planned to be built using Federal, State, and City of Yuma funds. The Fifth-Avenue location was selected because that was where the former entry to the Historical Army Quartermaster Depot was located, and it was close to the entry to Arizona from California. The welcome center would provide a one-stop location capable of meeting all visitor needs. This was good news to the Jaycees because it sounded like a perfect fit. In the meantime, the airplane was to be housed in the Bet-Ko-Air hangar. A partnership was formed and a plan of action was approved in 2002. The city government agreed to purchase the land for the new welcome center and help with its development. The Yuma Visitors Bureau agreed to operate the center once it was constructed. It was anticipated that the State of Arizona would play an important role in the construction of the building.

In 2005, The Jaycee Foundation agreed to donate the *City of Yuma* endurance flight airplane to the Yuma Crossing National Heritage Area Corporation. The ownership of the airplane was transferred via Federal Aviation Administration papers.

Crew removing wings to move airplane to firehouse in Yuma for storage.

Crew pushing fuselage onto trailer for move to storage area.

In 2006 the airplane was moved from the Bet-Ko Air hangar to Firehouse No. 3 for temporary storage. One year later, it was moved to a more permanent storage area until the completion of the welcome center.

Money for the design of the welcome center was made available in 2007. The design of the building called for the airplane to hang thirty-five feet high inside a building with glass walls on three sides. The fourth (south) side would be a simulated control tower eighty-five feet high, complete with an outside observation platform. The complete riverfront development from the quartermaster depot to the prison can be seen from this tower. The airplane can also be seen by people traveling in cars on Interstate 8 and on the Fourth Avenue Bridge. Upon completion, runway marking lines and lights will lead into and from the welcome center. The overall effect will simulate "The *City of Yuma* Flying Home."

The economic meltdown that started in late 2007 has had a major impact on all facets of life in Yuma and Arizona. The state subsequently withdrew funding for the welcome center because of a shortfall in revenue, and currently there are no other identified funds.

Why Not Celebrate Every Year?

In 2008 Jeannine Rhea, manager of the local Hampton Inn and a member of the Yuma Visitors Bureau, became aware of the *City of Yuma* record flight and wondered why Yuma didn't celebrate that accomplishment every year as an attraction to help tell the Yuma story. She spoke to various organizations, such as the Rotary Club, and the idea was well received. She decided to make a go of it and started holding meetings with interested people. It was a little late to plan for 2008, so she set her sights on 2009, the sixtieth anniversary, and every year afterward. A number of service organizations expressed interest in being a part of the celebration. Chapter 590 of the Experimental Aircraft Association (EAA) was the first to sign on, with Paul Rachels in charge. Their part will be to organize an aircraft fly-in similar to the famous Oshkosh fly-in in Wisconsin, which brings in thousands of aircraft from around the world. The Yuma Fly-in is on the schedule and commitments have been received from many locations—including Alaska and Switzerland. Members of the Aeronca Association are planning to attend, including Burt Rogers of Chugiak, Alaska, who owns the FAA-type certificate for the AC-15 Aeronca Sedan. Mr. Rogers has plans to start production of new Aeronca Sedans in the near future. Six Aeronca Sedans like the *City of Yuma* are expected to attend the Yuma Fly-in.

Jeannine and Tina Clark of the Yuma Crossing Heritage Foundation submitted paperwork for a federal grant to fund the efforts for a yearly celebration of Endurance Days. The request was rejected.

Jeannine decided to step down in March 2009. Yvonne Peach volunteered to take over and head up this effort. In April the first meeting was held. One cloud on the horizon at that time was the pending vote on the continuation of the two percent hospitality tax. Without passage of this measure, participation of the Visitors Bureau and other organizations was in doubt. The continuation was passed in May, and planning for a subdued sixtieth anniversary was resumed. Early planning called for the celebration to be held on October 10, starting with an EAA fly-in and pancake breakfast featuring the Aeronca Association at the Lux Air Jet Center FBO at Yuma International Airport. This will be followed up with a celebration downtown at the Historic Yuma Theater and the Yuma Art Center. A dinner will be held at the Crossing Park that evening.

The downtown events will start off with a showing of the 1929 Howard Hughes movie, *Hell's Angels*. This movie was originally shot without sound. Subsequent to shooting, Howard Hughes decided that he wanted sound on the film, and he tasked associate H. W. "Hub" Houston to get it accomplished. This was no small task since it had never been done before and was a first for the film industry. It took Hub and his crew a year to get the sound strip synchronized perfectly to the film at a cost of 1.7 million dollars. Howard Hughes liked the job so much that he gave the off-shoot company to Hub. The two men first became associated in 1925 at the Hughes Tool Co., Houston, Texas, when Hub was twenty-eight and Hughes was twenty.

Houston, who had less than an eighth grade education, started selling photo machinery to many giants in the United States and foreign movie and photo finishing industries in 1927. In fact, Houston equipment was used in the filming of *Hell's Angels* that same year.

In the 1960s, Hub Houston came to Yuma to visit his son, John Sam, who had a photo-processing contract with the U.S. Army Yuma Proving Ground to develop 70 mm Cinetheodolite film. This film was used to provide trajectory data for projectiles and parachute loads dropped from aircraft. Hub liked Yuma so much that he decided to move his operation from Los Angeles to Yuma. In 1972 he was named Arizona's small businessman of the year by the Small Business Administration.

In addition to the showing of *Hell's Angels*, a second movie of Howard Hughes' life, *The Aviator*, will be shown.

The ASU and PBS documentary, *Arizona Stories: Flight of the City of Yuma* will also be shown in a closed loop.

Chapter Seven

Yuma Sixty Years Later

As the title of this book implies, the story covers sixty years of Yuma history, from 1949 to 2009, from the inception of the idea to publicly promote the assets of Yuma, to today. This idea was implemented in an effort to ultimately entice the Department of the Army to keep the U.S. Army Yuma Test Branch open and convince the Department of the Air Force to reopen the World War II army air base. This effort was successful in that both the U.S. Army and the U.S. Air Force moved back into Yuma in 1951, eventually making both facilities permanent installations that still exist today.

The Yuma Flight Made the Difference

There are those who say that there is no correlation between the flight of the *City of Yuma* and the decisions to move the army and air force back into Yuma. But one must counter that argument with the fact that the Department of Defense had hundreds of other surplus posts and air fields that could have been selected, but they weren't. It is more than coincidence that two facilities in Yuma were reopened when many others were subsequently being closed. The WWII army air base in Blythe is an example. In 1949, Yuma and Blythe were almost mirror images of each other with lots of airspace, land space, and unused World War II army bases. Both were located on the banks of the Colorado River sixty miles apart. Both cities had similar climates and environments. Both depended on agriculture and tourism for their livelihood, although Blythe did have a U.S. Gypsum Sheetrock plant located nearby which produced Sheetrock for construction. Both had railroad lines and both were located on major east-west highways—Blythe on U.S. 69/70 and Yuma on the Bankhead Highway (U.S. 80.) The main difference between the cities was that the people of Yuma had the vision to develop legs so that they could walk into the future. They did this by developing and implementing a plan to get worldwide attention to the excellent flying and working conditions in the Yuma area. Newspapers all over the world had coverage of the flight. This flight reinforced to the decision-makers that Yuma was a place to get work done. The assets of Yuma were a perfect match to meet the requirements of the two installations. Both are now major installations under the Department of Defense. The U.S. Army Yuma Proving Ground with its multitude of test ranges blossomed into a premier range and is a member of the Major Range Test Facility Base (MRFTB) where the majority of items used by warriors in combat are tested. It also is a training facility that duplicates real world environments. Millions of direct labor test man-hours are accomplished there every year.

The Marine Corps Air Station (MCAS) is unique with its many ranges and long runways. MCAS Yuma is the busiest air station in the Marine Corps and the third busiest in the naval service. Its primary mission is to support aerial training for the Atlantic- and Pacific-fleet marine forces and navy and to serve as a base of operations for Marine Aviation Weapons and Tactics Squadron 1 and Third MAW units to include Marine Aircraft Group 13. MCAS, combined with other assigned areas in the Yuma area, allows training that duplicates real battlefield environments.

The Yuma airport of 1949 was little used. The Yuma International Airport of today is a joint-use facility shared with the MCAS and is capable of handling any aircraft in the world. You can stand in your front yard and watch Marine tactical aircraft and heavy transports loaded with Marines going to war. The picture on the back cover of this book, courtesy of Laryl Hancock of www.laryl.com, gives a visual of the types of aircraft that use this airport. It shows a replica of a 1930s mail plane, the *City of Yuma*, and an Air Force vintage B-52H (60-0037) *Wham Bam II*, a veteran of several combat missions.

The impact of these decisions on the Yuma area can best be told in a brief comparison of Yuma in 1949 and in 2009. Yuma, in 1949, had a population of approximately nine thousand people; by 2009 the population had grown to approximately 110,000. In the winter, the population swells by approximately eighty thousand to one hundred thousand winter visitors and up to thirty-five thousand produce workers. Area-wise, the city is twenty times larger. One high school served Yuma in 1949. In 2009 seven high schools exist to handle students from the same areas served in 1949. Blythe, on the other hand, remains pretty much as it was in 1949. The U.S. Gypsum Plant closed many years ago.

It goes without saying that, yes, all the efforts of those many involved in this story were well worth it.

END

About the Authors

Shirley Woodhouse Murdock

Shirley Woodhouse Murdock's brother, Bob, was one of the pilots in the Longest Flight. Both parents and her husband became pilots in the 1940s as well, and her two sons are pilots. Shirley's husband, George, and sons, Kenny and Jimmy, are farmers in Roll, Arizona, on the farm where she grew up.

Jim Gillaspie

Jim Gillaspie, native of New Mexico, graduated from the University of Arizona with a BSME degree. He began his aviation career in the U.S. Navy with the Naval Parachute Unit and later served in VFA-195 aboard the USS *Oriskany*. After navy life, he worked for the U.S. Army for twenty-eight years, primarily in Research, Development, Test, and Evaluation.

BIBLIOGRAPHY

ABC Affiliate, TV Channel 15, Phoenix. *Arizona Short Stories.* June 1998 (Interviews, Jim Gillaspie and Horace Griffen).

Arizona Republic. Main headline. October 12, 1949.

Beatty, Morgan. *NBC News of the World,* October 1949.

Bilingual Times, Taipei Times, September 20, 1999.

Bones, R.J. KTTI Radio, Yuma, March 13, 1999 and April 14, 1999.

Chicago Tribune, October 11, 1949.

Davis, Joel. *Yuma Daily Sun.* August 24, 1999, October 6, 1999, and October 11, 1990; and Que Pasa Calendar, supplement to the *Yuma Daily Sun,* "Flyin' High," October 9, 1999.

Gillaspie, Jim. *Arizona Flyways,* October 1999, cover, 6–7, 13.

Gillette, Frank M. *Pleasant Valley.*

Hoffmeyer, Fred. *Farm Credit Bio News Southwest,* Winter 1999, 1, 6–7.

Mabery, Chuck. *Yuma Daily Sun.* September 8, 1996.

Majure, David. KAET, Channel 8 TV, Phoenix, *Arizona History Collection of Arizona Stories, Season III,*   aired numerous times, beginning October 28, 2008.

Marries, Dan. KYMA-TV, Yuma, March 13, 1999.

Munson, Russ. "Hang Time." *Flying, Hang Time,* February 2000, 66–69.

Murdock, Shirley. *Buick Bugle* and book review, December 1996. *Ten-Ten*, 24–27 and back cover.

McCool, Lewis. *Durango Herald,* October 5, 1999.

O'Leary, Michael. *Air Classics* 39, no. 5 (June 2003): 20–22.

Phipps, John. *Talk of Yuma*, KJOK Radio, Yuma. Interviews, April 14 and 16, 1997, October 10, 1997, March 14, 1999.

Reinhold, Ruth M. *Sky Pioneering: Arizona in Aviation History,* 126–130, 182–183.

River Currents, Yuma Crossing National Heritage Area periodical, *The Legacy of the City of Yuma Endurance Flight,* August 2001.

Sanchez, Kim. KTTI and KBLU Radio, Yuma, 45-minute taped interview. May 1947.

Smith, Pam. *Yuma Daily Sun.* Numerous articles in 1949, 1999, and December 24, 2003.

Spencer, Ron. Yuma Jaycee Foundation newsletter, *Captain's Korner,* various issues.

Taylor, Reese H. *On Tour,* December 1949, 3–7.

Various *Yuma Daily Sun* articles beginning April 1941.

Vujovich, Elias J. *Invention and Technology* 20, no. 1 (Summer 2001): 5.

Wellton-Mohawk Kiwanis Club Calendar, 2000, cover.